THE
HALOGEN OVEN
COOKBOOK

THE HALOGEN OVEN COOKBOOK

Paul Brodel and Carol Beckerman

APPLE

A Quintet Book

First published in the UK in 2012 by
Apple Press
7 Greenland Street
London NW1 0ND
United Kingdom

www.apple-press.com

ISBN: 978-1-84543-447-2
QTT.HOCB

This book was conceived, designed, and produced by
Quintet Publishing Limited
6 Blundell Street
London N7 9BH
United Kingdom

Food Stylist: Maud Eden
Photographer: Ria Osborne
Art Director: Michael Charles
Designer: Melissa Alaverdy
Project Editor: Alison Hissey
Editorial Director: Donna Gregory
Publisher: Mark Searle

Quintet Publishing would like to thank Andrew James, Flavorwave, Morningware Inc., Coopers of
Stortford and JML for the supply of halogen ovens.

10 9 8 7 6 5 4 3 2 1

Printed in China by 1010 Printing International Ltd.

CONTENTS

Introduction

A halogen oven does almost everything in one pot that it normally takes a conventional oven, hob and grill to manage. It can bake, roast, sauté, steam, fry and grill – and it will do it better. All you have to do is plug it into a normal household electrical socket, and you are good to go!

A halogen oven is a fan oven, which combines the speed of a conventional oven with the instant heat of a halogen bulb to cook food more efficiently. It is basically a large glass bowl on a stand with a lid. The lid has a fan and an intense heat source – a halogen-heated lamp. It is small enough to sit on your worktop and large enough to feed a family of four comfortably. A very versatile piece of equipment, a halogen oven cooks slightly quicker and certainly more economically than conventional methods.

A halogen oven costs only a fraction of the sum of a conventional oven. As fuel costs rise, preheating a large conventional oven, even just to grill or bake for 30 minutes, becomes more expensive. A halogen oven almost never needs to be preheated. The amount of electricity needed to cook dinner is greatly reduced, so you save money in the long term.

Your halogen oven is also a much healthier cooking option. Overall you need far less fat to cook in a halogen oven than in a conventional oven or a frying pan on the hob. But food isn't dry – moisture is locked in, while the fat tends to melt away, resulting in healthy and delicious meals.

Halogen ovens really excel with roasting and grilling. Chicken roasted in a conventional oven will often dry out, but cooked in

your halogen oven, it will be moist and full of flavour. Red meat will be cooked to perfection, and bacon will be crispy. Fish is wonderful cooked in the halogen oven, as the flesh holds together beautifully and is moist and flavourful. The halogen oven is also great for quick dishes such as toasted sandwiches, especially those including cheese, so no need for expensive toasted sandwich makers any more.

Many vegetables are successfully cooked in the halogen oven, though some cook better than others. Porous Mediterranean vegetables such as courgette and aubergine bake beautifully, staying tender with a chargrilled edge, while dense root vegetables such as carrots and swede are best boiled on the hob, unless you cut them into julienne strips. Though potatoes are a root vegetable, they seem to be the exception, and, cooked in the halogen oven, you will get rave reviews for them every time. Whether roasted, baked or cooked as chips, they will be browned and crispy on the outside and soft and fluffy on the inside.

The whole family, but children especially, will enjoy the fast food aspect of halogen cooking, as burgers and bacon cook really quickly. You will find that a bacon sandwich in the morning for breakfast is not nearly so time-consuming with your halogen oven. Another way to save time and effort with a halogen oven is

to grill your meat or fish on the top rack while baking or steaming your vegetables on the lower rack, and you can even cook meals all in one dish.

The halogen oven is incredibly versatile, and you will be amazed at the baked treats it can produce. Sweet creations such as luscious chocolate desserts will be meltingly soft and exquisite, and cinnamon rolls will be airy, delicate and fluffy. Just swap the baking tins that you would normally use for large cakes for smaller and individual tins, which are more appropriate for the cooking style of the halogen oven. With a few changes here and there, you will

discover alternative methods for cooking all your favourite recipes in the halogen oven.

Whether you use your halogen oven in conjunction with your conventional oven, or do all your cooking in it, it will prove itself invaluable in creating diverse and delicious meals to wow your friends and family. The halogen oven is officially no longer a fad, or a temporary blip on the kitchen horizon, it is here to stay, and the recipes in this book will inspire you to get the most out of it for every meal.

Buying a Halogen Oven

The most important thing to do when buying a halogen oven is to look at all the models available, and uncover as much information as you can. First, decide how you will use your halogen oven. Will it completely replace a normal oven, or will you use it along with the rest of your kitchen equipment?

Second, consider how many people you will be cooking for. Depending on the size of your oven, you can cook a complete meal for two or three, or parts of a meal, such as the meat or potatoes, for four to six people. As halogen ovens come in different sizes, decide which is the right size for your needs. If you are cooking for just one, you may think the very smallest is best. But look at the capacity of the oven. If you want to cook a whole chicken, it may be a good idea to buy a larger size, as it is better to have one slightly too big than too small. Consider also that the larger the oven, the bigger will be the pans you can fit into it, so it will be more versatile.

Third, because you need to plug the halogen oven into a nearby electric socket, decide where the best location in the kitchen would be. The cable connects to the lid, which is where the motor is. That means when you lift the handle, the oven will automatically switch off, and you can remove the lid to either place it on a heatproof mat, or straight onto a specially designed lid stand (which can be purchased either with the oven or as an optional extra). The cable will still be plugged in, so you need enough space nearby to put the lid down. Some ovens have a lid that is hinged onto the glass bowl. If yours is one of these, you will need to make sure you have room above the oven to raise the lid, without it hitting anything above.

Finally, consider whether you want to select an oven that has extra accessories included in the price or whether you would prefer to purchase them separately, as needed. The extras available are an extender ring, which raises the height of the lid and enables you to cook a larger bird; a diffuser, which is a perforated tray sometimes used for steaming or covering a dish to prevent it burning; toast racks; and a lid stand.

THINGS TO CONSIDER

- **Will you use your halogen oven alone or alongside a regular oven?**

- **How many people do you usually cook for?**

- **What types of foods do you usually cook?**

- **What extra accessories do you need?**

Equipment

To fit your halogen oven to your needs, a range of extra accessories can be bought that have been specially designed for halogen oven cooking. These will ensure that your oven is perfectly suited to the types of foods you like to prepare.

Most halogen ovens come complete with an oven tray, and two racks, one high and one low. These are loose and just placed in the bottom of the glass bowl. The low one has short legs, which sit it close to the bottom, leaving a bigger gap between the rack and the lamp. The high one has longer legs, which puts it closer to the lamp. As a general rule, if the food is dense, use the low rack and cook for a longer time on a higher heat, and if the food is porous or very thin, cook on the high rack on a lower heat for a shorter period of time.

You will also need oven gloves and long tongs to move food around inside the oven and turn it over while it is cooking.

You will need a baking dish that will fit comfortably inside the oven, so there is room for the fan to move hot air around the dish in order to cook the food inside. Over time you will build up a collection of baking tins that are the ideal size for your own particular halogen oven.

You will find ordinary ramekin dishes invaluable for a great number of different recipes. You can use them for individual soufflés or desserts. You can put paper or silicone cups for muffins inside them, and even cook individual cinnamon or bread rolls. If using paper or silicone bakeware, make sure to place it only on the lower rack to prevent burning, and check regularly.

Foil can be used to make little parcels for cooking food. This is especially useful for cooking fish, because it will decrease cooking smells. You can also lay foil on the rack and place food directly on it, which makes clean-up faster.

Halogen Cooking Techniques

As with anything new, cooking in the halogen oven takes a little practice to perfect. The following is a guide to essential techniques that will help you to get the best results from your oven.

Temperatures and Timings

The symbols to the right of each recipe title give an indication of how long the recipe will take to prepare and cook. Times are in minutes unless otherwise stated.

 Preparation time: 5 minutes

 Cooking time: 10 minutes

While temperatures and timings specified in recipes are as accurate as possible, ovens from different manufacturers can vary significantly. In order to determine whether your oven cooks more or less quickly than average, before using your oven you should carry out the 'Tortilla Test'.

Even when you know your oven well, it is a good idea to check on your food as it cooks. If you find that food is burning on the surface, either lower the temperature or move the food to the lower rack if it is on the high one. You can also cover the food with foil. You can pierce the foil to let steam out, if you wish. Using foil will lengthen the cooking time slightly.

Most food will cook best when turned over a few times during the cooking process, but in a halogen oven you will not need to keep basting it with oil. In particular, if you want to cook a larger piece of meat, such as a whole chicken, you must turn it over a few times to allow it to cook all over. Cakes and rolls will also benefit from being turned over during baking.

THE TORTILLA TEST

Follow the breakfast tortilla recipe (page 37), using the exact temperature settings listed in the instructions, and checking on the tortilla regularly as you cook it. It will be clear when it is cooked, as the egg will have set and become opaque. If the time needed to reach this stage is longer than listed in the recipe, you will need to increase the cooking times listed in this book accordingly. If less time is needed to reach this stage, decrease cooking times accordingly. So if your halogen oven cooks the tortilla 10% quicker than stated in the recipe, decrease cooking times by 10%, and vice versa.

The heat from the lamp will brown dishes very quickly, but placing a bowl of water in the base of the oven will help prevent this. You can also cover the item with foil or the diffuser, turn the heat down, or move the item from the high rack to the low rack, if necessary.

When the cooking time has finished, remove the food immediately to prevent build-up of moisture in the oven. If you need to keep food warm, turn the heat down to about 15°C (60°F) for a short time.

Grilling

The halogen oven is ideal for grilling. As a general rule, use the high rack, but if you are cooking meats that spit, place them on the lower rack. This will prevent the fat spitting upwards onto the heating lamp, which is delicate and could be damaged. Place foil in the base of the oven to catch the fat.

Roasting

To roast meat, brush it with a little vegetable oil and place in a roasting tin. You can also cook meat directly on one of the racks, which has the benefit of the fat melting away. Place the oven tray or foil underneath to catch the drips of fat. If you want to be completely sure that meat is cooked properly, check the temperature of the meat with a meat thermometer.

Steaming

There are two ways to steam food in the halogen oven. For foods that are quick to steam, place the food on the lower rack of the oven and place the round oven tray on the upper rack. Fill the round tray with boiling water. Turn the oven to 250°C (480°F); the light will vaporise the water and the fan will move it around.

Alternatively, place the food in an ovenproof casserole dish or make a foil package; add a couple of tablespoons of water, lemon juice or good-quality stock; and cover.

Cooking Vegetables

Many vegetables are ideal for steaming. To roast raw vegetables, cut them into small cubes or slices, about 1–2 cm (½–1 in) in size, brush with vegetable oil, and place them on the oven tray on the high rack. Thicker vegetable slices should be cooked on the lower rack. Root vegetables will take the longest.

Vegetables often take longer to cook than meat, so if you want the vegetables to be ready at the same time as other food, you will need to start cooking them first. This is especially true for root vegetables, and carrots in particular.

TURNING

Halogen Ovens are great for many reasons, but despite the name the cooking itself is closer to grilling than baking. This means you'll need to turn some food to ensure even cooking.

- **Pay close attention to turning instructions in the recipe**

- **Always use tongs when handling hot food**

- **If buying a new halogen oven, make sure it is big enough to turn food easily – consider buying a medium or large size rather than a small oven**

Approximate Cooking Times

The following cooking times listed here are intended as a guide only. Much depends on the thickness of the food being cooked, the size of your halogen oven, and whether there is anything else in the oven cooking at the same time.

	Baking
SINGLE LAYER CAKE	Low rack with extender ring, 35 to 45 minutes at 175°C (350°F).
CUPCAKES	Low rack with extender ring, 25 to 40 mins at 175°C (350°F).
LOAF OF BREAD	Low rack 13 minutes on each side at 200°C (400°F).
BREAD ROLLS	Low rack 15 to 25 minutes (depending on size) at 215°C (420°F).

	Vegetables
HARD VEGETABLES	Low rack 30–40 minutes at 200°C (400°F).
SOFT VEGETABLES	Low rack 15–20 minutes at 200°C (400°F).
ROOT VEGETABLES	Par boil first, then 45 minutes at 200°C (400°F), high rack.
JACKET POTATO	Low rack 25–40 minutes at 110°C (225°F).
ROAST POTATOES	Par boil first, then 45 minutes at 200°C (400°F), high rack.
CHIPS	High rack 10 minutes at 200°C (400°F)

	Roasted Meats
CHICKEN Small (1–1.5 kg/2–3 lb) Medium (1.5–2 kg/3–4.5 lb)	Low rack 45 minutes at 215°C (420°F), then 45 mins at 175°C (350°F). Turn every 10–15 mins. Low rack 45 minutes at 215°C (420°F), then 55 mins at 175°C (350°F). Turn every 10–15 mins.
LAMB JOINT (1.5 kg/3 lbs.)	Low rack 240°C (460°F) for 20 minutes, turning after 10 minutes, then 60 minutes at 175°C (350°F) turning every 15 minutes. For a well-done joint, continue cooking for up to 30 minutes more.
PORK JOINT (1 kg/2 lbs.)	Rub with salt prior to cooking. Low rack. 215°C (420°F) for 60 minutes, turning every 15 minutes, then 175°C (350°F) for 30 minutes.
BEEF JOINT (1 kg/2 lbs.)	Low rack 240°C (460°F) for 30 minutes, turning every 10 minutes, then 175°C (350°F) for 10 minutes (rare/blue), 30 minutes (medium), or 50 minutes (well done).

	Grilled Meats
STEAK	High rack 250°C (475°F). Rare: 2–5 minutes each side; Medium: 5–7 minutes each side; Well-done: 7–10 minutes each side.
PORK CHOPS	High rack 200°C (400°F), 6–8 mins each side
BACON	High rack 220°C (425°F), 4–6 mins
SAUSAGES	Low rack 135°C (275°F), 10–12 mins
CHICKEN BREAST	High rack 190°C (375°F), 12–15 mins
FISH (fillet portion)	Low rack 200°C (400°F), 10–12 mins
FISH (whole)	High rack 250°C (480°F), 6–12 mins each side

Care and Cleaning

Read your manufacturer's instructions for your particular oven, and always allow the bowl to cool before you clean it, as cold water may crack the hot glass.

Some ovens have a self-cleaning or wash setting, but if yours does not, these are the directions: After letting the oven cool, remove any small bits of food and pour off any oil or fat left in the glass bowl. Put 5–10 cm (2–4 in) of cold water in the bottom of the bowl, add a little washing up liquid and set the temperature to 15°C (60°F). Turn the timer to 10 or 15 minutes. The bulb will heat the water inside, and the fan will swirl the water around the bowl. This should result in a sparkling clean bowl. Pour off the soapy water, rinse with cool water and dry with a clean cloth. Do not use abrasive cleaners or scouring pads on the glass bowl. You may leave the oven racks and oven tray in the oven during the cleaning process, which will loosen any particularly grimy bits, before washing them in the sink as normal.

Safety Advice

Keep the halogen oven on a stable heatproof surface, away from the edge. Make sure there is a suitable electric socket nearby, so that the cord does not hang over the edge of the work surface or touch anything hot while in use. Do not plug any other appliances into the same socket while you are using the halogen oven, and do not move the oven while it is in use.

Only use the halogen oven inside, and never on the hob or in a conventional oven.

The lid is very heavy. Make sure you have space and a heatproof mat immediately next to the oven, so that you can lift the lid off the glass bowl and place it straight onto the mat. If you have a stand for the lid, make sure it is on a flat heatproof surface, not near the edge, and has plenty of space around it. If your oven's lid is hinged onto the glass bowl, be certain you can raise the lid without letting it hit anything above.

All the electrics are in the lid, so do not place the lid in water.

The bowl gets very hot during use, especially at the top near the lamp, so have tongs and oven gloves to hand to lift food from the oven.

Do not use plastic in the oven. Only use ovenproof tins, baking dishes, foil or the oven tray made for halogen ovens. Use silicone or paper muffin cases with caution.

Do not turn the timer backwards, as this will damage it. If the timer is still running, and you need to turn off the oven, simply lift the handle, which works as an on/off switch. You should always use the handle to lift the lid on and off the glass bowl.

Always make sure the lid is securely attached to the glass bowl before switching on the oven.

If any faults develop, contact the retailer or the manufacturer.

BREAKFAST

Almond French Toast with Crispy Bacon

French toast always makes a great breakfast. In this recipe, the flavour of almonds blends beautifully with maple syrup and bacon, making a delicious combination.

8 strips bacon
75 g (3 oz) cups sliced almonds
2 large eggs
70 ml (2½ fl oz) whole milk
2 tbsp maple syrup, plus extra for
    serving
1 tbsp dark rum or Grand Marnier
    (optional)
4 (1 cm/½ in-thick) slices from a
    large brioche or challah loaf
    (or use 8 smaller slices)
3 tbsp unsalted butter
icing sugar, to serve

Serves 4

Lay the strips of bacon on the oven tray and cook in the halogen oven on the high rack at 190°C (375°F) for about 3 minutes each side, until crispy. Remove from the tray and keep warm while you make the French toast. Wipe any remaining bacon grease off the oven tray.

Spread the sliced almonds in a thin layer on a large plate. In a large shallow bowl, whisk the eggs and milk together. Add the maple syrup and rum (if using) and whisk again. Soak 1 slice of bread in the egg mixture and press lightly on top of the almonds. Turn over and press the other side into the almonds. Repeat with the other 3 slices. Melt half the butter on the oven tray on the high rack at 175°C (350°F) for 1–2 minutes, until foaming. Place two of the bread slices on the oven tray at a time, and cook on the high rack for 1 minute, turn the slices over, and cook for 3 minutes. Carefully turn again, and cook for another 2 minutes, or until golden brown and the nuts are slightly crispy at the edges. Watch carefully to make sure the almonds do not burn. Keep warm while you cook the other two slices, adding the extra butter as necessary.

Serve 1 slice of French toast per person, sprinkled with a little icing sugar, and with 2 strips bacon.

ANOTHER WAY

Substitute white soda bread or raisin bread, and serve with whipped cream and fresh mixed berries instead of bacon and maple syrup. You could also substitute pecans or other nuts for the almonds, or dispense with them altogether.

Overnight French Toast with Caramelised Apples

This is such a great dish for holidays. When you have a houseful of guests, prepare it the night before, and amaze everyone with a delicious breakfast, seemingly effortlessly.

50 g (2 oz) cup butter, softened
100 g (4 oz) cup brown sugar
2 medium-size tart apples,
    peeled, cored and sliced
3 eggs
170 ml (6 fl oz) milk
1 tsp vanilla extract
6–7 slices French bread, cut on
    the diagonal
1 tbsp sugar
1½ tsp ground cinnamon
½ tsp ground nutmeg
icing sugar and maple syrup,
    to serve

Serves 4–5

Make the caramelised apples. In a large frying pan, melt the butter over medium heat, add the sugar and cook for a minute. Add the apples, turn them over to coat them with butter and sugar and continue to cook over medium heat until the apples are tender and the sugar is slightly caramelised, about 5 minutes. Transfer to a 23 cm (9 in) shallow baking dish, and set aside to cool completely.

In a large bowl, whisk together the eggs, milk and vanilla extract. When the apples have cooled completely, dip the slices of bread in the egg mixture and place them on top of the apples in a single layer. Spoon the rest of the egg mixture over the bread.

In a small bowl, mix together the sugar, cinnamon and nutmeg, and sprinkle half on top of the bread. Cover and chill for 8–24 hours.

To cook, remove the cover and set the dish on the low rack of the halogen oven. Cook for 15 minutes at 165°C (325°F). Turn the slices over, sprinkle the remainder of the spiced sugar over the top and cook for 10 minutes more. Remove from the oven, place each portion on a plate and serve sprinkled with icing sugar on top and maple syrup on the side.

ANOTHER WAY

To make the recipe extra-rich and creamy, substitute 3 tbsp double cream for 3 tbsp milk.

To make Peach–Pecan French Toast, replace the apples with sliced peaches and add 65 g (2½ oz) chopped pecans.

Welsh Cakes

These little spiced currant cookies are normally cooked on a griddle; in the halogen oven they do not take long to bake, so watch them carefully.

300 g (10 oz) flour
1 tsp baking powder
1 tsp pumpkin pie spice
pinch salt
100 g (4 oz) butter or margarine
100 g (4 oz) plus 2 tbsp
    caster sugar
100 g (4 oz) currants
1 egg, lightly beaten
1–2 tbsp milk, as needed

Makes 20–25

In a large bowl, sift the flour, baking powder, pumpkin pie spice and salt. Cut in the butter, either with a pastry cutter or with your fingers, until the mixture resembles fine breadcrumbs. Add the sugar and the currants, and mix until combined. Add the egg and mix to a soft dough, adding a little milk, if needed. Roll out to 6-mm (¼ in) thickness and cut into rounds with a 6-cm (2½ in) plain cutter. Place on the oven tray, and bake in batches on the high rack of the halogen

ANOTHER WAY

Try making the Welsh cakes thicker, then, when cooled, split and spread with butter and fruit conserve for a more filling treat.

oven at 220°C (425°F), for 2–3 minutes each side. Transfer to a wire rack to cool. Serve, or store in an airtight container.

Breakfast Bars   +25

If you do not have time in the morning for a proper breakfast, grab a halogen-oven-baked breakfast bar and eat on the go! These are delicious and wholesome at the same time.

100 g (4 oz) butter
2 tbsp honey
200 g (7 oz) brown sugar
450 g (1 lb) rolled oats
40 g (1½ oz) sultanas
40 g (1½ oz) chopped
    macadamia nuts
a pinch of salt

Makes 12 bars

In a medium saucepan, melt the butter and honey, add the sugar and cook for 3 minutes over a gentle heat, until the sugar has dissolved. Add the oats, sultanas, macadamia nuts and salt, and stir well to combine. Transfer to the baking tin, and cook in the halogen oven on the low rack at 165°C (325°F) for 10 minutes. Turn the heat down to 135°C (275°F), and cook for a further 30 minutes, until a lovely golden brown. Remove from the oven. Leave to cool in the tin for 5 minutes before cutting. Cool in the tin for another

ANOTHER WAY

Melt 200 g (7 oz) dark chocolate in a bowl over hot water, add 1 tbsp sunflower oil and stir gently. Spread over the breakfast bars. Leave to cool before serving.

10 minutes, then transfer the bars to a wire rack to cool completely. Store in an airtight container.

Almond Biscotti

These little cookie slices show just how versatile your halogen oven can be. Double-baked until crisp, they are just perfect to be dunked in coffee, as they soften beautifully without falling apart.

125 g (5 oz) flour
1 tsp baking powder
¼ tsp salt
1 egg
100 g (4 oz) sugar
2 tbsp sunflower oil
1 tsp almond extract
50 g (2 oz) finely chopped
   blanched almonds

Makes 18–20

In a large bowl, sift together the flour, baking powder and salt. In the bowl of a freestanding mixer, beat the egg and sugar together until light and fluffy. Add the sunflower oil and almond extract, and beat until combined and the mixture is thick and smooth. Reduce the speed and add the flour mixture. Finally, fold in the chopped almonds.

Turn the dough onto a floured work surface, flour your hands and divide the dough in half. Transfer one half to a plate, cover and keep cool. Transfer the other half to the oven tray, and mould it into a smooth log, 18 cm (7 in) long, 6 cm (2½ in) wide, and 1.5 cm (¾ in) high. Place on the high rack of the halogen oven and bake at 165°C (325°F) for 10 minutes, turn it over, and bake for another 10 minutes, or until light brown and slightly puffed. Remove from the oven and carefully cut the log on a slight diagonal into 1.5 cm (¾ in)-wide slices. Return to the oven's low rack, and bake for 4 minutes. Turn them over and bake for another 4 minutes, or until the cut surfaces of the biscotti have browned slightly and are dry to the touch. Transfer to a wire rack to cool completely, while you repeat the process with the other half of the dough. These can be stored for several days in an airtight container.

ANOTHER WAY

Add 25 g (1 oz) chopped dried cranberries to the dough before baking, and dip the end of the biscotti in melted dark or white chocolate for an extra-special treat.

Blanched almonds are almonds with their skins removed. It is great fun and very satisfying to blanch them yourself. Just put them in a medium bowl and cover with boiling water. Leave for 2 minutes only, drain and slide and pop the skins off. They should slide off easily.

Glazed Cinnamon Rolls

The subtle tangy flavour of sour cream and lemon in the pastry dough contrasts beautifully with the sweetness in the glaze. These rolls are a little tricky to bake in the halogen oven because you have to flip them over, but they are actually much better, because they stay so soft and light.

125 ml (4 fl oz) warm milk
   (43°C/110°F)
4 tbsp plus 1 tsp sugar, divided
1 packet dry yeast
250 g (10 oz) bread flour
½ tsp salt
½ tsp baking soda
1 small egg
1 tsp vanilla extract
zest of 1 lemon
2 tbsp sour cream
½ tsp vegetable oil, plus extra
   for greasing
2 tbsp butter, plus extra for
   greasing and brushing
50 g (2 oz) dark brown sugar
1 tsp ground cinnamon

Soft Icing
125 g (5 oz) icing sugar, sifted
2–3 tbsp milk
½ tsp glycerine (optional; it
   keeps the icing soft)

Makes 9

Grease a 20 cm (8 in) square cake tin with a little butter.

Dissolve 1 tsp sugar in the warm milk and sprinkle the yeast on top. Set aside for 10–15 minutes until frothy. In a large bowl, mix together the flour, salt, baking soda and 4 tbsp sugar. In a small bowl, whisk the egg, vanilla, lemon zest and sour cream together. Make a well in the centre of the flour and pour in the egg and sour cream mixture and the yeast liquid. Work to a soft dough, adding a little more milk if the dough feels too dry, or a little more flour if it feels too sticky. Turn dough out onto a lightly floured surface, and knead until you have a soft, smooth and elastic dough. Alternatively, knead the dough in a freestanding mixer for 5 minutes.

Grease a bowl with the vegetable oil. Place the dough in the greased bowl, turning it so that it is coated in oil all over, cover and leave to rise in a warm place for about an hour, until it has doubled in size.

In a medium bowl, combine 2 tbsp butter with the brown sugar and cinnamon. When the dough has doubled, turn out onto a lightly floured surface, knock back, knead lightly and roll out to a 30 x 15 cm (12 x 6 in) rectangle. Spread the butter and sugar mixture evenly over the surface, leaving a small margin around the edges. Roll tightly into a cylinder, sealing the far edge well. Turn the cylinder so that the seam is underneath,

ANOTHER WAY

If your halogen oven is too small to fit a 20 cm (8 in) square tin, put the rolls in greased ramekins and bake in batches, but still turn them over halfway through cooking.

and cut into 9 equal-sized slices about 3 cm (1¼ in) thick. Arrange the slices, touching, in the greased cake tin, cover and leave to rise in a warm place for about 30 minutes. Brush the buns with a little melted butter, place the tin on the low rack in the halogen oven and bake at 150°C (300°F) for 10 minutes. Turn the buns out upside down onto a baking sheet, then in one quick motion, slide them back into the tin, brush with a little more melted butter and bake for another 10 minutes, or until golden brown. Leave to cool in the tin for 5 minutes, then transfer to a wire rack, placing them close together.

In a small bowl, beat the icing sugar and just enough milk to make a smooth icing. Add the glycerine if using. Spread icing over the buns while they are still warm, allowing a little to run down the edges. Best served right away, while still warm.

Bacon Bagels

Homemade bagels are a real treat and much easier to make than you think. They are a dense bread, and, with the bacon for protein, will easily keep you going until lunch.

1 tsp sugar
250 ml (8 fl oz) warm water (43°C/110°F)
1 packet dry yeast
350 g (12 oz) bread flour, plus extra for kneading
1 tsp salt
vegetable oil, for greasing
16 strips bacon
salt and freshly ground black pepper
tomato ketchup, to serve

Makes 8

Dissolve the sugar in the warm water, add the yeast and leave until frothy, about 10–15 minutes.

Sift the flour and salt into the bowl of a freestanding mixer, make a well in the centre and add the yeast liquid. Using the dough hook of the mixer, knead for 5 minutes. If the dough seems too sticky, add a little more flour; if it seems too dry, add a little more warm water. You need a firm but soft dough. Place in a greased bowl, turn the dough over to coat it all over, cover and leave to rise for about an hour, or until doubled in size. Knock back and divide into 8 pieces. Roll each piece in your hands until it is perfectly round, then gently push your finger into the middle to make a hole, and twirl it around on your finger a little to widen the hole. Place on a baking sheet, cover and leave to rise for about an hour.

Fill a large pan with about 7.5–10 cm (3–4 in) of water, and bring to the boil. Drop in the bagels, 2 or 3 at a time. They will rise to the surface almost immediately. Cook for 1 minute on each side, or 2 minutes if you prefer a chewier bagel. Using a slotted spoon, remove

ANOTHER WAY

Before baking the bagels, brush them with beaten egg white and sprinkle with fennel or poppy seeds, then serve with cream cheese and smoked salmon, instead of bacon and ketchup.

bagels from the water and place on the greased oven tray. Bake on the low rack of the halogen oven at 200°C (400°F) for 6–7 minutes, flip them over with a spatula and cook for 6–7 minutes more. When done, they should be a lovely golden brown colour. Transfer to a wire rack to cool.

While the bagels are cooling, grill the bacon in batches on the oven tray in the halogen oven on the high rack at 200°C (400°F) for 3–4 minutes per side, or until cooked and crispy. Drain on paper towels. To serve, split the bagels in half, add the bacon (2 strips per bagel), a little tomato ketchup, and season with salt and pepper. Serve immediately.

Carrot and Potato Hash Browns with Pancetta

This twist on the classic hash brown recipe is delicious with fried eggs and baked Boston beans.

1 large potato, peeled and grated
1 medium carrot, peeled and grated
½ medium onion, peeled and grated
1 medium egg
1 tbsp flour
¼ tsp dried mixed Italian herbs
salt and freshly ground black pepper
1 tsp olive oil, divided
30 g (1 oz) diced pancetta

Serves 4

Dry the grated potato, carrot and onion with kitchen paper. Place in a large bowl. Mix in the egg, flour and dried herbs. Season with salt and pepper. Wipe the round oven tray with half the olive oil. Divide the potato–carrot mixture into quarters. Place them on the tray and form into circles, pressing down on them to get out all the air. Drizzle with the remaining olive oil. Place the diced pancetta around the hash browns. Cook on the low rack of the halogen oven for

ANOTHER WAY

Children love these tasty hash browns, and you could even add other vegetables to them to make a really healthy breakfast.

12 minutes at 230°C (450°F), then turn over the hash browns and place back in the oven for an additional 11 minutes.

Oven-Baked Rosti

A rosti is like a small pancake but is made of coarsely grated potatoes and onions. Baking in the halogen oven is a really healthy way to make rostis. They are delicious as a breakfast dish with fried eggs and bacon.

350 g (12 oz) coarsely grated peeled
    raw potatoes
50 g (2 oz) coarsely grated raw
    onion
1 egg
1 tbsp flour
salt and black pepper
2 tbsp vegetable or olive oil

Makes 4 rosties

Pat dry the potatoes and onion with some kitchen paper and place in a large mixing bowl. Mix in the egg and flour, then season with salt and pepper. Divide into 4 equal parts and shape into 4 burger-sized patties.

Pour half the oil onto the oven tray and place the 4 patties on the tray. Place on the low rack in the halogen oven, drizzle with the rest of the oil and cook at 260°C (500°F) for 12 minutes. Turn the rostis over and cook for an additional 12 minutes until golden brown. Serve hot.

ANOTHER WAY

Rather than hand-grating the potatoes for the rosti, it is much quicker and easier to use a grater attachment on an electric mixer.

Meat-Lovers' Potato Grill

Nothing grills as quickly as a halogen oven, which makes it ideal for preparing this recipe. The chorizo really helps to add flavour to the potato when cooking. Serve with fried eggs and grilled tomatoes.

1 large potato, peeled and diced
½ medium onion, sliced
2 chorizo sausages, sliced
2 strips bacon, chopped
1 tsp olive oil
salt and freshly ground
    black pepper
1 slice thick-cut ham, sliced
    into strips

Serves 2

In a large bowl, mix the potato, onion, chorizo, bacon and olive oil. Season with salt and pepper.

Tip mixture onto the round baking tray and set it on the low rack in the halogen oven. Cook at 230°C (450°F) for 25 minutes, stirring every 7 minutes. Add the ham strips, stir and cook for 2 minutes more. Remove and serve.

NOW TRY THIS...

THREE PEPPER BREAKFAST HASH

Follow the recipe as directed above, adding ½ red pepper, ½ yellow pepper and ½ green pepper, diced, along with the chorizo and bacon.

SPICY SWEET POTATO GRILL

Follow the recipe as above, substituting sweet potato for the white potato. Make the dice slightly larger than you would for white potato. Omit the bacon and ham, and instead add 1 small red chilli, chopped and deseeded, and 1 small courgette, chopped, along with the chorizo. Cook as directed above.

SMOKED SALMON GRILL

Follow the recipe as above, omitting the onion, bacon and chorizo, and instead adding in 1 spring onion, finely chopped, along with the potato. Cook for 25 minutes, stirring every 7 minutes, then add 1 slice smoked salmon, chopped. Cook for 2 minutes more. Serve with scrambled eggs, with sour cream dip (page 114), if liked.

VEGETARIAN POTATO GRILL

Follow the recipe as directed above, omitting the chorizo, bacon and ham. Add in ½ red pepper, ½ medium courgette, diced, 125 g (5 oz) button mushrooms and 1 tsp Italian seasoning along with the potatoes and onions.

Sausage Patties

Shop-bought sausage patties contain a lot of salt and fat. It is so much healthier to make them yourself, as you can control the ingredients. All you need to go with these patties is plain or cheese scones and a few slices of ripe tomato.

750 g (1½ lb) premium low-fat
   minced pork
½ tsp ground white pepper
½ tsp ground ginger
½ tsp ground sage
1 tsp dried mixed Italian herbs
2 tsp salt, or to taste
30 g (1 oz) breadcrumbs
freshly ground black pepper
scones and tomato slices,
   to serve

Serves 6

In a large bowl, using your hands, combine all the ingredients together, making sure that the herbs and spices are distributed evenly. Still using your hands, form the sausage meat into 6 patties, pressing the meat firmly together. You can use a hamburger press for this, if you have one. If you prefer small patties, make 12. Place them on the oven tray, sprinkle with some freshly ground black pepper and cook on the high rack of the halogen oven at 200°C (400°F) for 4–6 minutes. Turn them over, sprinkle with some more pepper and cook for another 4–6 minutes, or until cooked through. Cook in batches if necessary. Serve immediately.

NOW TRY THIS...

TURKEY PATTIES

Mix 750 g (1½ lb) minced turkey, 1 small diced onion, 1 tbsp chopped fresh parsley, 2 cloves garlic, ½ tsp ground white pepper, 2 tsp salt, ½ tsp ground ginger, ½ tsp red chilli flakes and 30 g (1 oz) breadcrumbs. Mould the mixture into patties and cook as directed above.

APPLE AND MAPLE SAUSAGE PATTIES

Follow the sausage patties recipe as above, omitting the mixed Italian herbs and adding 1 medium apple, peeled, cored and finely chopped, 2 tbsp maple syrup, and ¼ tsp cinnamon when you mix together the ingredients. Cook as directed above. Serve with scones and crispy bacon.

SAUSAGE PATTIES WITH ONION GRAVY

The patties are delicious with onion gravy for dinner. Follow the recipe as directed above to make the patties. To make the gravy, gently fry 2 sliced large onions in a little oil for 15 minutes. Add 1 tsp flour and 1 tsp Dijon mustard and cook for 2 minutes. Gradually add 250 ml (8 fl oz) good-quality beef stock and 1 beef stock cube. Season and simmer until thickened. Serve with the patties and mashed potatoes.

Spanish Tortilla

This is a basic Spanish tortilla, but feel free to add some different ingredients, such as peas, chopped red pepper, ham, chorizo, fresh tomato or cheese.

1 large potato, peeled and cut
    into small cubes
½ onion, sliced
1 tbsp butter
1 tbsp olive oil
4 medium eggs
1 tbsp milk
1 tbsp water
salt and freshly ground
    black pepper

Makes 4–6 slices

In a medium saucepan, boil the cubed potato for 6 minutes in boiling water, then drain and set aside.

Place a cup of boiling water into the base/glass bowl of the halogen oven. This helps to slow down the browning process.

Place the sliced onion on the round oven tray with the butter and oil.

Cook on the low rack in the halogen oven at 260°C (500°F) for 6 minutes. Add the potatoes, mix well and cook for 5 minutes more.

In a small bowl, mix the eggs with the milk, water, salt and pepper. Pour the egg mixture over the potatoes. Lower the heat in the halogen oven to 150°C (300°F) and cook for 12 minutes. Slice and serve hot or cold.

NOW TRY THIS...

HAM AND CHEESE

Follow the recipe as above, adding 30 g (1 oz) chopped deli ham, 30 g (1 oz) cheddar cheese and 30 g (1 oz) diced tomato to the egg mixture. Cook as directed above.

SPICY SAUSAGE

Follow the recipe as above, adding 30 g (1 oz) chopped chorizo and ½ red pepper, diced, when you add the onions. Cook as directed above.

VEGETABLE FEAST

Follow the recipe as above, substituting ½ small red onion for the white onion. Add ½ red pepper, diced, ½ courgette, diced, 4 mushrooms, sliced and 30 g (1 oz) frozen peas along with the onions.

MEAT FEAST

Follow the recipe as above, adding 8 slices pepperoni, 30 g (1 oz) cubed deli ham and 30 g (1 oz) cubed cooked chicken to the egg mixture. Cook as directed above. Serve with tomato sauce (page 59).

BROCCOLI AND STILTON

Follow the recipe as above, adding 30 g (1 oz) crumbled stilton, and 30 g (1 oz) parboiled broccoli torn into very small florets, to the egg mixture. Cook as directed above.

LUNCH

Turkey Pie

This is a great way to use up that leftover turkey from a roast. If you ever thought it was complicated to make a turkey pie, this recipe will prove you wrong!

Pastry
200 g (8 oz) plain flour
125 g (5 oz) butter, cold (slice a
**   bit to fit into processor)**
1 tbsp water
1 beaten egg, for glazing

Filling
1 medium onion, chopped
4 mushrooms, sliced
2 tsp olive oil
1 tbsp butter
salt and freshly ground
**   black pepper**
150 ml (5 fl oz) whole milk
1 tbsp cornflour
325 g (11 oz) cooked turkey
**   (cubed)**
150 ml (5 fl oz) double cream
1 chicken stock cube mixed with
**   4 tbsp boiling water**
1 tbsp freshly chopped parsley

Serves 4

To make the pastry, place the flour, cold butter and 1 tbsp water into a food processor fitted with a mincing blade. Mix until the pastry forms a ball. Wrap the pastry in plastic wrap and chill in the refrigerator for 30 minutes.

To make the filling, put the chopped onion, mushrooms, olive oil, butter and seasoning into a baking dish or deep pie tin. Place dish on the low rack in the halogen oven and cook at 260°C (500°F) for 12 minutes, stirring twice during cooking.

Meanwhile, in a mixing bowl, mix a little of the milk with the cornflour to dissolve it, then stir in the cubed turkey. Mix in the remaining milk and the cream, stock and parsley. Pour the mixture into the dish, stir to combine with the onions and mushrooms and cook for 10 minutes. Remove and stir.

Roll out the pastry to the size of the dish, place it on top of the filling and brush with the beaten egg to glaze. Cook at 260°C (500°F) for 12 minutes or until golden brown. Serve immediately.

ANOTHER WAY
Add 1 tbsp chopped fresh tarragon to the filling for a very flavourful variation. You can also use this pastry as a topping for any number of different pie fillings.

Asian-Spiced Chicken Wings

This recipe will be a big hit and will bring you rave reviews. You could make extra sauce to serve with the wings, if you want.

1/5 kg (3 lb) chicken wings
2 cloves garlic, minced
½ tsp salt
2 tbsp soy sauce
2 tbsp hoisin sauce
3 tbsp honey
1 tsp sesame oil
2 pinches cayenne pepper
freshly ground black pepper
1 spring onion, green part only,
    finely chopped
1½ tbsp sesame seeds

Serves 4–8

With some kitchen shears, snip off the tips of the chicken wings and halve the wings at the joint. If desired, remove as much skin as you can.

In a large bowl, mix together the crushed garlic, salt, soy sauce, hoisin sauce, honey, sesame oil and cayenne pepper. Add the chicken wings to the bowl, and turn around to coat all over. Season with plenty of freshly ground black pepper. If you have time, place in the refrigerator to marinate for an hour or so. Transfer the chicken wings to the round oven tray, and cook on the high rack of the halogen oven at 450°F for 10 minutes, turning every 2–3 minutes. Turn the temperature down to 230°C (400°F) and cook for 10–15 minutes more, or until cooked through, turning halfway through cooking time. Remove from the oven and stir in the spring onion and sesame seeds. Serve immediately.

NOW TRY THIS...

THAI WINGS

Mix 1 tbsp fish sauce with 250 ml (8 fl oz) coconut milk, zest and juice of 1 lime, 2 shredded kaffir lime leaves (optional), 1 bashed lemongrass stalk, 2 deseeded and sliced Thai chillies and 2 sliced spring onions. Marinade 1.5 kg (3 lb) chicken wings for an hour, then cook as for Asian-Spiced Chicken Wings.

CARIBBEAN WINGS

Mix 2 tbsp red wine vinegar, 1 large grated onion, 2 tbsp tomato purée, 4 crushed garlic cloves, 2 tsp brown sugar, 1 very finely chopped habanero chilli, and 2 tsp anchovy paste. Marinade 1.5 kg (3 lb) chicken wings overnight, and cook as directed above.

HOT WINGS

Mix 1 tbsp paprika with 1 tsp each of salt, garlic salt, cayenne pepper, lemon pepper, white pepper and ground cumin. Rub into 1.5 kg (3 lb) wings. Marinate for 15 minutes, then cook as directed above. Melt 250 ml (8 fl oz) chilli sauce with 250 g (9 oz) butter, 1 tsp each garlic salt and cayenne pepper, and mix to combine. Pour over cooked wings and toss.

HERBY WINGS

Mix 125 ml (2½ fl oz) olive oil with 2 tbsp balsamic vinegar, 2 tbsp fresh parsley, 1 tbsp chopped fresh rosemary, ½ tbsp chopped fresh lemon thyme, and salt and pepper. Marinate for 1 hour in the refrigerator and cook as directed above.

Chicken and Corn Enchiladas

Sautéed chicken and vegetables are wrapped up in tortillas before being baked in enchilada sauce, then topped with cheese. Make the dish as spicy as you like by varying the amount of chilli in the sauce.

Enchilada Sauce
1 tbsp vegetable oil
1 medium onion, finely chopped
2 cloves garlic, minced
1 tsp chilli powder, or to taste
400 g (14 oz) tin chopped tomatoes
    in sauce
125 g (5 oz) tin tomato purée
1 beef stock cube
2 tsp sugar
12 g (½ oz) freshly chopped coriander
salt and freshly ground black pepper

Enchilada Filling
1 medium onion, finely chopped
75 g (3 oz) aubergine, 1 cm (½ in) cubes
75 g (3 oz) courgette, 1 cm (½ in) cubes
½ red pepper, 1 cm (½ in) cubes
8 cherry tomatoes
2 tbsp vegetable oil, plus extra for
    greasing
3 boneless and skinless chicken breasts,
    cut into 2.5 cm (1 in) pieces
1 tsp chilli powder
2 tsp ground coriander
2 tsp ground cumin
12 g (½ oz) freshly chopped coriander
1–2 tbsp freshly chopped basil
1 red chilli, seeded and finely chopped
200 g (8 oz) tin baby sweetcorn, drained
275 g (11 oz) can baked beans in sauce

To Finish
1 tsp olive oil
8 15 cm (6 in) tortillas
200 g (8 oz) grated cheddar cheese
sour cream and chopped spring onions,
    to serve

Makes 8

Make the enchilada sauce. In a large saucepan, heat the oil, add the onion and cook for 5 minutes, until slightly softened. Add the garlic and cook over a gentle heat for 10 minutes. Add the chilli powder and cook for 1 minute, stirring continuously. Add the tomatoes, tomato purée, stock cube and sugar. Cover and simmer for 25 minutes. Add the coriander and season with salt and pepper. Transfer to a bowl and set aside.

Make the filling. Place the vegetables on the oven tray, drizzle with a little vegetable oil and place on the low rack of the halogen oven. Bake for 10 minutes at 200°C (400°F), turn the vegetables over and cook for a further 5–10 minutes, or until they are slightly charred on the edges and tender. Remove from the oven and place in a large bowl.

In a large frying pan, heat 1 tbsp oil. When it is hot, but not smoking, add the chicken and sauté for 10 minutes, until browned and cooked through. Add the chilli powder, coriander and cumin, and cook for 1 minute, stirring continuously.

TIP
Sealing the tortillas by frying them in a little oil means they will not soak up too much of the sauce.

Add chicken to the charred vegetables, and mix in the coriander, basil, red chilli, sweetcorn and baked beans.

Wipe the pan, add 1 tsp oil and fry each tortilla for 1 minute per side, adding a little more oil as necessary. Lay the tortillas on the work surface. Spoon about 5–6 tbsp of the chicken and vegetable filling into the middle of each tortilla. Roll up tightly and place side by side in a greased baking dish. Spoon enchilada sauce on top, and sprinkle with cheddar cheese. Cover and cook on the low rack at 175°C (350°F) for 30 minutes, then remove the lid and cook for another 10 minutes, or until piping hot and nicely browned on top. Sprinkle with chopped spring onions and serve with sour cream.

Chicken Fajitas with Pico de Gallo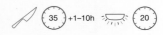

These are delicious and authentic-tasting fajitas and the Pico de Gallo is a great accompaniment.

Pico de Gallo

8 ripe plum tomatoes, deseeded
    and chopped
1 small red onion, finely
    chopped
2 cloves garlic, crushed
1 jalapeño pepper, halved
    and deseeded
1 tbsp olive oil
juice of 1 lime
5 tbsp freshly chopped
    coriander
salt and freshly ground
    black pepper

Marinade

60 ml (1¼ fl oz) honey
60 ml (1¼ fl oz) soy sauce
2 tsp dried basil
2 tsp dried oregano
1 tbsp tomato ketchup
2 tbsp brown sugar
2 tbsp olive oil
2 tbsp red wine vinegar
1½ tsp ground ginger
freshly ground black pepper
4 skinless and boneless chicken
    breasts
½ tsp salt
1 tsp chilli powder

For the Fajitas

2 red peppers, finely sliced
2 green peppers, finely sliced
2 large onions, finely sliced
8–10 flour tortillas, warmed
sour cream, to serve

Serves 4

Put all the ingredients for the Pico de Gallo in a medium bowl, mix well and chill for at least 8 hours.

Prepare the marinade. In a medium bowl, combine the honey, soy sauce, basil, oregano, ketchup, brown sugar, olive oil, red wine vinegar, ground ginger and pepper. Place the chicken on a plate, and season with the salt and chilli powder. Slice the chicken into strips, place it in the marinade and turn it around to coat it all over. Chill for 1–10 hours. Remove chicken from the marinade, place the marinade in a small saucepan and bring to the boil. Remove from the heat and transfer to a small bowl. Place the chicken on the oven tray on the high rack of the halogen oven, drizzle with a little marinade and cook at 220°C (425°F) for about 8 minutes, turning the chicken over occasionally, and basting with the marinade. When no longer pink in the middle, remove from the oven and keep warm. Place the peppers and onions in a shallow baking dish, and cook on the high rack for about 8 minutes at 230°C (450°F), stirring occasionally, and basting with a little marinade. When the peppers and onions are tender, transfer the chicken to the baking dish, stir to combine with the pepper and onion and return to the halogen oven on the high rack. Cook for 5 minutes at 175°C (350°F), or until piping hot and slightly charred on the edges. Divide the chicken and peppers between the tortillas, and roll up. Serve with the Pico de Gallo, and the sour cream on the side.

ANOTHER WAY

Add guacamole to serve on the side. Mix 2 peeled, pitted and chopped avocados with 2 tsp lemon juice, 1 tsp Worcestershire sauce, 2 cloves crushed garlic and 2 tsp each of dried red chilli flakes and minced fresh onion.

Jerk Chicken with Mango Salsa

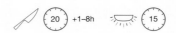

This Caribbean recipe is meant to be fiery, but you can reduce the amount of chile for a milder version. Don't omit it altogether though; this recipe brings out the chile flavor as well as the heat.

Jerk Seasoning
1 tbsp. ground allspice
4 cloves garlic, peeled and
    crushed
1 tbsp. canola oil
2 scotch bonnet chiles
1 tsp. black pepper
a pinch of salt
1 tsp. ground coriander seeds
1/2 tsp. ground cinnamon
1 tsp. ground ginger
2 tsp. chili powder
juice of 1 lime
1/2 tsp. garlic powder

Jerk Chicken
1 tbsp. mayonnaise
6 chicken thighs, boned and
    skinned

Mango Salsa
1 mango, peeled, pitted, and
    finely chopped
2 green onions, finely sliced
2 tomatoes, deseeded and diced
juice of 1 lime
1 tbsp. chopped fresh cilantro
1 jalapeño pepper, chopped

Serves 4

Place the jerk seasoning ingredients into a food processor and blend thoroughly. In a bowl, mix 1 tbsp. jerk seasoning and 1 tbsp. mayonnaise, then add the chicken thighs, coat, and allow to marinate for at least 10 minutes in the refrigerator (overnight is even better).

Cook in a round oven tray on the high rack of the halogen oven at 400°F for 7 minutes each side or until cooked, turning halfway though the cooking time.

For the mango salsa combine all the ingredients and serve with the jerk chicken.

TIP

The remaining jerk seasoning will keep in a sealed container in the refrigerator for up to two weeks.

Tuna Melt

This potato and tuna melt makes a fantastic, warming lunch on a chilly day. Nothing can be more comforting than seeing the cheese bubble under the intense halogen light.

4 medium baking potatoes
1 tsp. olive oil
1/4 tsp. salt
1 cup drained canned tuna
4 green onions, finely chopped
3 tbsp. mayonnaise
1 tbsp. tomato ketchup
1/4 tsp. paprika (smoked is good)
2 tbsp. freshly chopped parsley
1/2 cup shredded cheddar cheese
    or Swiss cheese

Serves 4

Wash and dry the potatoes, prick them with a fork, rub with the oil, and sprinkle with salt. Place them on the low rack of the halogen oven and cook at 450°F for 45–70 minutes, depending on the size of the potatoes or until cooked. Turn over every 15 minutes.

When cooked, slice potatoes in half lengthwise. Scoop out the pulp into a mixing bowl. Add the tuna, onions, mayonnaise, ketchup, paprika, and parsley. Mix well. Fill the potato skins with the mixture, and sprinkle with the grated cheese. Cook the potatoes on the high rack at 450°F for 5 minutes or until golden brown.

ANOTHER WAY

Potatoes baked in the halogen oven are delicious with any number of fillings. Try substituting cubed ham or canned salmon for the tuna.

Steak Burgers with Mozzarella Cheese

A hamburger made with good-quality meat can be just as good as a steak. Mixing rump steak with a cheaper cut keeps the hamburger moist and the cost down.

225 g (9 oz) rump steak
225 g (9 oz) braising steak
1 tbsp olive oil, plus extra for
    greasing
½ small onion, finely chopped
25 g (1 oz) finely grated
    Parmesan cheese
25 g (1 oz) chopped parsley
1 tsp dried mixed Italian herbs
salt and freshly ground
    black pepper
1 small egg, lightly beaten
100 g (4 oz) mozzarella cheese

Makes 4

Cut the meat into cubes, trimming off any large pieces of fat. Chop or mince the meat and put into a large bowl.

In a small frying pan, heat 1 tbsp olive oil, add the onion and sauté until softened, about 5 minutes. Add the onion to the beef, along with the Parmesan cheese, parsley, Italian herbs, salt and pepper. Using your hands, bind the mixture together with the egg. Divide the mixture into 8 portions and shape them into patties with your hands. Place 4 patties on a work surface. Slice the mozzarella cheese into 4 parts, and place a slice on each of the 4 patties. Top with the remaining patties and seal the edges well to prevent the cheese from oozing out.

Grease the oven tray and place the hamburgers on it. Set the tray on the high rack of the halogen oven and cook at 220°C (425°F) for 5–6 minutes. Turn the patties over and cook for another 5–6 minutes, or until lightly browned and cooked through. Serve immediately.

TIP

If you mince the meat yourself, handle it as little as possible, and you will be rewarded with a tender hamburger with a delicious flavour. Try to avoid chopping the meat in a food processor, as it is very easy to overwork the meat, which makes it tough.

Beef Cannelloni in Tomato Sauce

A rich Italian dish, cannelloni is pasta rolled around a delicious meat sauce, covered with tomato sauce and baked in the oven.

vegetable oil, for greasing
500 g (1 lb 2 oz) minced beef
1 large onion, finely chopped
2 cloves garlic, crushed
1 400 g (14 oz) tin chopped tomatoes
   in sauce
1 125 g (5 oz) tin tomato purée
80 ml (2 fl oz) good-quality beef stock
1 beef stock cube
1 tsp sugar
1 tsp dried mixed Italian herbs
salt and freshly ground black pepper
8 dried lasagne sheets
2 tsp cornflour, mixed with a
   little water
2 cups tomato sauce (page 59)
finely grated Parmesan cheese, to serve

Serves 4

Grease a baking dish with a little vegetable oil. In a large saucepan, dry-fry the beef until browned, then drain off and discard the fat. Return the beef to the saucepan, add the onion and garlic and cook for 10 minutes, until the onion has softened. Stir in the tomatoes, tomato purée, stock, stock cube, sugar, herbs, salt and pepper. Cover, and simmer gently for 40 minutes. Add the cornflour mixture to the meat sauce, stirring continuously. Simmer for 5 minutes, remove the pan from the heat and leave to cool for 10 minutes.

While the beef is simmering, bring a large saucepan of water to the boil, and cook the lasagne sheets for 10 minutes. Drain and refresh in cold water.

ANOTHER WAY

For a variation, add 50 g (2 oz) ricotta cheese and 30 g (1 oz) fresh spinach leaves to the meat sauce, and sprinkle with grated cheddar cheese before baking.

Place 2 tbsp meat sauce on each cooked lasagne sheet, and roll up tightly. Place them side by side in a baking dish. Ladle over the tomato sauce, cover with a lid or foil and bake on the low rack of the halogen oven at 175°C (350°F) for 35 minutes, until piping hot. Sprinkle with a little Parmesan cheese before serving.

Philly Cheese Steak

The intense radiant heat of the halogen oven helps to cook and brown the meat very quickly, making this another fast and easy everyday recipe that is great for a tasty, filling lunch.

1 onion
1 green pepper
1 tbsp oil
½ tsp garlic salt
½ tsp coarsely ground
   black pepper
150 g (6 oz) rib-eye steak
4 slices provolone cheese
2 burger buns, halved

Serves 2

Thinly slice the onion and pepper, and place in a bowl. Add the oil, garlic salt and pepper, and mix. Tip mixture onto the round oven tray and place in the halogen oven on the low rack. Cook at 260°C (500°F) for 5 minutes.

Thinly slice the steak and add to the round tray, stir, and cook for a further 8 minutes at 260°C (500°F), stirring every 2–3 minutes.

ANOTHER WAY

For a delicious taste variation, stir in 2 tbsp sweet chilli sauce in the last 2 minutes of cooking.

Put 2 slices cheese into each bun. Add the beef mixture and serve hot.

Quesadillas with Refried Beans

Cooked in the halogen oven, this traditional Mexican recipe will make a delicious treat for all the family in no time at all.

½ red onion, sliced
½ tbsp olive oil
150 g (6 oz) refried beans
4 flour tortillas
1 tomato, diced
½ red pepper, sliced
1 jalapeño pepper, sliced
    and deseeded
75 g (3 oz) cooked diced
    chicken
4 tbsp grated cheddar cheese
salt and freshly ground
    black pepper

Serves 2

Place the red onion with the olive oil on the round oven tray on the low rack in the halogen oven. Cook at 260°C (500°F) for 5 minutes. Pour in the refried beans, mix and cook for 3 minutes or until thoroughly heated. Remove and pour into a bowl.

Place a flour tortilla on a clean round oven tray. Spread half of the refried beans on the tortilla. Top with half the diced tomatoes, half the peppers and jalapeño, half the chicken and half the cheese. Place on the low rack and cook at 260°C (500°F) for 6 minutes, then add another tortilla wrap on top to form a sandwich. Cook for

1 minute more. Remove from the oven and keep warm while cooking the other quesadilla.

Slice into quarters like pizza and serve with lettuce and sliced tomato.

NOW TRY THIS...

CUBAN SANDWICH QUESADILLA

Spread the bottom tortilla with a thin layer of American mustard, then add 1 slice deli ham, 1 slice roast pork, 1 thinly sliced dill pickle and 1 slice Swiss cheese. Grill on the low rack at 260°C (500°F) for 6 minutes, before adding another tortilla on top, and cooking for 1 minute more.

.

QUESADILLAS DE CARNE

Follow the recipe as above, substituting 30 g (1 oz) cooked minced beef, seasoned with salt and black pepper, for the cooked chicken. Serve with shredded lettuce and slices of avocado and tomato.

CORN QUESADILLAS

Follow the recipe as above, omitting the refried beans, and instead spreading the tortillas with 2 tbsp mayonnaise mixed with 1 tbsp lime juice. Add 175 g (7 oz) fresh sweetcorn kernels along with the diced tomato. Cook as directed above.

Mini Quiches

This is a very useful pastry for any type of quiche, and it's so simple to make it in a halogen oven.

Shortcrust Pastry
150 g (6 oz) plain flour
125 g (5 oz) salted butter
pinch salt
1 tbsp cold water

Quiche Filling
3 eggs
60 ml (1¼ fl oz) milk
2 tbsp double cream
100 g (4 oz) grated cheddar
    cheese
3 strips bacon, chopped
¼ medium onion, chopped
salt and freshly ground black
    pepper
1 tomato, sliced

Serves 3

To make the shortcrust pastry, put the flour, butter and salt into a food processor. Process until the mixture has the consistency of fine breadcrumbs, then mix in the cold water until a dough is formed. Wrap the dough in plastic wrap and chill for 20 minutes, then remove it from the fridge and divide it into 3 balls. On a lightly floured surface, roll out each ball into a circle.

Lightly grease 3 ramekin dishes, then line each one with a circle of pastry. With a fork, prick the pastry in the bottom of the dishes a couple of times. Then place a sheet of baking paper, topped with baking beans (for baking blind), in each ramekin. Place the ramekins on the low rack of the halogen oven and cook at 200°C (400°F) for 20 minutes.

Meanwhile, beat the eggs in a bowl. Add the milk, cream, grated cheese, chopped bacon and chopped onion. Mix and season well with salt and pepper.

When the pastry has finished cooking, remove the dishes from the halogen oven and remove the waxed paper and baking beans. Pour the egg mixture evenly into the ramekins, place a slice of tomato on each one and sprinkle with more salt and pepper. Return the ramekins to the halogen oven on the low rack. Cook at 190°C (375°F) for 20 minutes, then 5 minutes more at 150°C (300°F). Serve immediately or leave to cool as desired.

NOW TRY THIS...

BROCCOLI AND BLUE CHEESE

Make up the quiche bases and mixture as above, adding 6 broccoli florets and 50 g (2 oz) crumbled blue cheese instead of bacon and cheddar. Cook as directed above.

SMOKED SALMON

Make up the quiche bases and mixture as above, but omit the grated cheddar cheese, bacon and onion, and add in 500 g (1 lb 2 oz) cream cheese and 100 g (4 oz) diced smoked salmon instead. Cook as directed above.

BRIE AND CRANBERRY

Make up the quiche bases as above. Place 3 slices of brie around the base of each, spread with 2 tsp cranberry jelly, then pour over the egg mixture, omitting the cheese, bacon and onion. Cook as directed above.

Croque Monsieur

The traditional French ham and cheese sandwich is ideal for cooking in the halogen oven. It will be crisp and golden on the outside and succulent on the inside.

6 tbsp finely shredded Swiss cheese, such as Gruyère

2 tbsp sour cream or crème fraîche

salt and freshly ground black pepper

½ tsp Worcestershire sauce

½ tsp Dijon mustard

4 slices white sandwich bread, buttered

2 thin slices deli ham

Makes 2 sandwiches

In a small bowl, mix the cheese with enough cream or crème fraîche for it to hold together. Add the seasoning, Worcestershire sauce and mustard, and mix until combined.

Place 2 slices of bread butter-side down on the oven tray. Divide the cheese mixture between them, and spread it right to the edges. Add the deli ham, cutting it to fit, if necessary. Cover with the other 2 slices of bread, butter-side up, to make 2 sandwiches. Press down lightly. Place the oven tray on the high rack of the halogen oven and cook at 200°C (400°F) for 3–4 minutes. Turn the sandwiches over and cook for 3–4 minutes more, or until golden brown on the outside and melting on the inside.

ANOTHER WAY

To make a Croque Madame, add a fried egg to the sandwich just before cooking.

Halloumi Kebabs

These Greek cheese kebabs are great if you have a vegetarian guest coming for dinner. They can be prepared in very little time in advance, then popped into the halogen oven to cook quickly and evenly. These kebabs are delicious with a salad and baked potatoes.

4 wooden skewers, soaked in hot water for 10 minutes before use

200 g (8 oz) halloumi cheese

½ red onion

16 sundried tomatoes in oil

1 small tin pineapple chunks, drained

Serves 2

Cut the cheese and red onion into cubes. Drain the tomatoes and reserve the oil. Alternate the halloumi, onion, sundried tomatoes and pineapple on the 4 soaked skewers. Place the skewers on the round baking tray and brush all over with 1 tbsp of the sundried tomato oil.

When ready to cook, place the baking tray on the low rack of the halogen oven. Cook for 15 minutes at 230°C (450°F), turning every 5 minutes. Remove and serve 2 skewers per person.

TIP

Soaking the skewers before use prevents the food from sticking to them, but more importantly, stops the wood skewers burning under the fierce halogen light.

Spicy Penne with Artichokes

The artichokes and sundried tomatoes add a flavour reminiscent of the Mediterranean to this spicy pasta dish. The tomato sauce is so versatile, it can be used with many of the dishes in this book. This is a great dish for vegetarians.

350 g (12 oz) dried penne pasta
80 g (3½ oz) quartered tinned
   artichokes
80 g (3½ oz) halved sundried
   tomatoes
25 g (1 oz) freshly chopped basil,
   plus more to serve
2 red chillies, deseeded and finely
   chopped, or to taste
freshly grated Parmesan cheese,
   to serve

Tomato Sauce
2 tbsp olive oil
1 large onion, finely chopped
2 cloves garlic, crushed
2 x 400 g (14 oz) tins chopped
   tomatoes in sauce
2 x 125 g (5 oz) tins tomato purée
2 tsp soy sauce
2 tsp Worcestershire sauce
2 tsp dried mixed Italian herbs
2 tsp sugar
salt and freshly ground
   black pepper
2 chicken or vegetable
   stock cubes

Serves 4

Make the tomato sauce. In a large saucepan, heat the oil. When it is hot but not smoking, add the onion and garlic, and cook over medium heat until the onion has softened, about 10 minutes. Add the tomatoes, cover, and simmer gently for 15 minutes. Add the tomato paste, soy sauce, Worcestershire sauce, Italian herbs, sugar, salt, pepper, and stock cubes. Simmer, covered, for 10 minutes. Remove from the heat and set aside.

Bring a large saucepan of water to a boil, and add the pasta. Cook according to the instructions, until just tender. Drain and tip back into the saucepan. Add the tomato sauce, artichokes, sun-dried tomatoes, basil, and chiles, and stir briefly to combine. Transfer to a casserole dish. Cook, covered with a lid or foil, on the low rack of the halogen oven at 375°F for 30–40 minutes, or until heated through. Serve sprinkled with a little Parmesan cheese and extra chopped basil.

ANOTHER WAY

If you prefer, you can add sautéed sliced chicken breast for extra protein. In a large frying pan, heat 2 tbsp vegetable oil, and add 450 g (1 lb) skinless and boneless chicken breasts, cut into 6 mm (¼ in) slices. Add 2 tsp Cajun seasoning (page 116) and sauté chicken for 10 minutes over medium heat. Add to the pasta just before serving.

Garlic Mushrooms

This is a great low-fat side dish to accompany grilled steak or chicken. The extra beef stock cube and garlic in the sauce intensify the flavour.

450 g (1 lb) mushrooms
2 cloves garlic, crushed
2 shallots, finely chopped
60 ml (2½ fl oz) good-quality
    chicken or beef stock
1 beef stock cube
salt and freshly ground
    black pepper
25 g (1 oz) freshly chopped
    parsley, to serve

Serves 4

Remove most of the stalks from the mushrooms, then halve the mushroom caps. Put them in a baking dish and add the garlic, shallots, stock and stock cube. Cook on the low rack of the halogen oven at 175°C (350°F) for 20–25 minutes, stirring the mushrooms every 5 minutes while cooking. Season to taste with salt and pepper, and serve immediately, sprinkled with parsley.

ANOTHER WAY

Substitute the chicken or beef stock for 60 ml (2½ fl oz) white wine, and use a mix of different varieties of mushrooms.

Ratatouille

This classic French dish works really well in the halogen oven. Roasting the vegetables first on the low rack caramelises them and helps to bring out the sweetness of the dish.

1 red onion, sliced
1 small aubergine, cubed
1 small courgette, sliced
2 large tomatoes, cut into wedges
1 yellow pepper, cut into large dice
1 clove garlic, chopped
2 tbsp tomato purée
1 tbsp olive oil
pinch mixed dried herbs
salt and freshly ground black pepper
400 g (14 oz) tinned chopped tomatoes
3 tbsp tomato ketchup
300 ml (12 fl oz) vegetable stock

Serves 6

In a large baking dish that can fit into the halogen oven, mix the red onion, aubergine, courgette, fresh tomatoes, yellow pepper, garlic, tomato purée, olive oil, mixed herbs and salt and pepper.

Place the dish in the halogen oven on the lower rack and cook at 225°C (440°F) for 20 minutes. Stir every 5 minutes as the vegetables begin to roast and caramelise.

Add the tinned chopped tomatoes, ketchup and vegetable stock. Mix well.

ANOTHER WAY

This dish can be spiced up with some fresh chillies or cayenne pepper. Topped with cheese, it also makes a tasty vegetable bake.

Lower the heat to 200°C (390°F) and cook for 20 minutes, stirring every 5 minutes. Serve hot.

Vegetable Spears with Parmesan Sprinkle

Cut all the vegetables into equal-sized pieces, add plenty of seasoning and a sprinkling of Parmesan for a delicious accompaniment to roast meat or casseroles.

1 medium carrot
2 medium parsnips
1 medium sweet potato
1 medium potato
1 raw beetroot
2 tbsp olive oil
1 tbsp dried rosemary
salt and freshly ground
    black pepper
2 tbsp finely grated
    Parmesan cheese

Serves 4

Peel and cut all the vegetables into equal-sized spears, 6 mm (¼ in) wide and about 5 cm (2 in) long. Drop them in the bottom of the glass bowl of the halogen oven, drizzle with olive oil, add the rosemary and season with plenty of salt and pepper. Bake at 230°C (450°F) for 30 minutes, or until lightly browned and tender. Stir occasionally. Serve sprinkled with Parmesan.

ANOTHER WAY

For a quick and easy dinner, slice 2 boneless and skinless chicken breasts, season well with salt and freshly ground black pepper, then tuck them among the vegetables as they cook. Check the chicken is cooked through before serving.

Baked Courgette

This is a very quick side dish to prepare. It is delicious with grilled meats.

2 medium courgettes
1 tbsp olive oil
salt and freshly ground
    black pepper
50 g (2 oz) grated Swiss cheese,
    such as Emmental

Serves 4

Top and tail the courgettes and cut into 6 mm (¼ in)-thick slices lengthways. Place on the round oven tray, brush the tops with oil and sprinkle with salt and pepper. Place in the halogen oven on the low rack and cook at 260°C (500°F) for 5 minutes per side. Sprinkle with the cheese and cook for a further 3 minutes. Remove from the oven and serve hot.

ANOTHER WAY

For garlic courgette, add 1 crushed clove of garlic to the oil before brushing the courgette. For herbed courgette, sprinkle with dried Italian mixed herbs or oregano. You can also use a different cheese, such as cheddar.

Squash and Sweet Potato Bake

This can be served as a side dish or as a vegetarian main dish.

1 red onion, sliced
1 small butternut squash, peeled,
    deseeded and cut in small cubes
1 sweet potato, peeled and cubed
2 cloves garlic, finely chopped
¼ tbsp celery salt
1 tsp dried thyme
2 tbsp olive oil
salt and freshly ground black pepper
1 tsp cornflour
2 tbsp water
375 ml (12 fl oz) double cream
50 g (2 oz) grated cheddar cheese

Serves 4

Place the red onion, butternut squash, sweet potato, garlic, celery salt, thyme, olive oil, salt and pepper in a large bowl. Mix well, then place in a baking dish. Set the baking dish on the lower rack in the halogen oven and cook at 260°C (500°F) for 20 minutes, stirring every 5 minutes.

Mix the cornflour with the water, then add the cream and stir. Pour this mixture on top of the roasted vegetables and cook at 260°C (500°F) for 5 minutes.

Sprinkle with cheese and cook at 175°C (350°F) for 15 minutes more. Serve hot.

ANOTHER WAY

To make this dish more substantial, add 125 g (5 oz) mushrooms, and serve with steamed vegetables. Add 25 g (1 oz) crumbled blue cheese with the cream for a stronger flavour.

Green Bean Casserole

This dish is often made with condensed mushroom soup, but it is so much healthier to make your own sauce. If you cannot find mushroom ketchup, substitute 1 tsp Worcestershire sauce and an additional 1 tsp soy sauce.

1 tsp vegetable oil, for greasing
500 g (1 lb 4 oz) thin green beans
   (such as French beans)
50 g (2 oz) butter
1 small onion, finely chopped
1 clove garlic, crushed
100 g (4 oz) finely sliced mushrooms
25 g (1 oz) flour
425 ml (14 fl oz) milk
2 tbsp mushroom ketchup
1 tsp soy sauce
1 chicken stock cube
salt and freshly ground black pepper
1 tbsp vegetable oil
1 large onion finely sliced
1 tbsp brown sugar
Parmesan cheese, to serve

Serves 6

With a little vegetable oil, grease a casserole dish that will fit inside the halogen oven.

In a large saucepan filled with boiling water, blanch the green beans for 5 minutes, drain and refresh with cold water. Set aside.

Melt the butter in the saucepan, add the onion and garlic and cook over a gentle heat for 10 minutes until softened. Add the mushrooms and cook for 5 minutes. Stir in the flour and cook for 3 minutes, stirring continuously. Gradually stir in the milk, incorporating it into the roux and vegetables slowly, then cook over a gentle heat until the sauce has thickened. Add the mushroom ketchup, soy sauce and chicken stock cube, stirring continuously. Taste the sauce, and season with a little salt and plenty of pepper. Put the drained beans into the casserole dish, pour in the mushroom sauce and place on the low rack in the halogen oven. Cook for 20–25 minutes at 175°C (350°F), or until heated through, stirring every 5 minutes to turn the beans around so that they heat up faster.

Meanwhile, in a large frying pan, heat the vegetable oil, and when it is hot but not smoking, add the sliced onion and cook over a

ANOTHER WAY

Make the mushroom sauce into a cheese sauce by omitting the mushrooms and mushroom ketchup, and substituting 100 g (4 oz) finely grated cheddar cheese and 1 tsp Dijon mustard. Also add 1 skinned, deseeded and chopped tomato and 25 g (1 oz) chopped spinach to the beans in the casserole dish before pouring in the sauce.

gentle heat for 15 minutes. Add the brown sugar and continue to cook for about 10 minutes. Turn the heat up to high and cook for 2 minutes, stirring continuously, until the onions have browned and are caramelised. Remove from the heat and keep warm.

When the beans are heated through, remove the casserole from the oven, tip the caramelised onions on top and serve immediately, sprinkled with a little freshly grated Parmesan cheese.

Focaccia

This is a very wet dough, so it is best when kneaded in a mixer with a dough hook. Any time you need to handle the dough, use oil instead of flour on your hands to prevent it from sticking. This bread needs to be started well in advance. The rye flour is used to add a bit of extra flavour, but normal wheat flour can be substituted.

½ tbsp fresh yeast or 1 tsp
    dried yeast
250 ml (8 fl oz) warm water
1 tsp sugar
200 g (7 oz) bread flour
1 tbsp rye flour
½ tsp salt
3 tbsp olive oil
1 tsp dried mixed Italian herbs

Makes 1 round loaf

Mix half the yeast with 200 ml (6 fl oz) water and ½ tsp sugar. Leave for 6 minutes.

Mix in 100 g (4 oz) flour and the salt, and knead for 5 minutes with the dough hook. Grease the dough ball with 1 tbsp olive oil, then place in a mixing bowl and cover with plastic wrap. Leave for 12 hours or overnight in a warm place.

After 12 hours, mix the remaining yeast with the remaining water and ½ tsp sugar. Leave for 6 minutes. Mix in remaining flour and knead for 5 minutes. Combine this dough with the first dough and knead for 5 minutes. Rub with 1 tbsp olive oil, place in the mixing bowl, cover with plastic wrap and leave to rest in a warm place for 2 hours.

Place on a greased round baking tray, cover with 1 tbsp olive oil and make indentations with your thumb about 20 times. Sprinkle the indentations with the dried herbs. Leave in a warm place to rise for 20 minutes.

ANOTHER WAY

This is delicious with the wilted spinach and cream cheese recipe (page 111), or just enjoyed on its own, dipped in a little olive oil.

Preheat the halogen oven to 260°C (500°F) for 3 minutes. Lower the heat to 175°C (350°F), place the baking tray on the low rack and cook for 25 minutes. Turn the bread over, raise the heat to 425°F, and continue to cook for 7 minutes. Remove and leave to cool until ready to serve.

DINNER

Mediterranean Roast Chicken

Lemon, rosemary and garlic are classic Mediterranean flavours. Cooking chicken with lemon brings out all its flavours and helps tenderise it.

1 (1.5–2 kg/3–4 lb) chicken,
    washed and patted dry
1 lemon, halved
1 tbsp olive oil
1 tbsp chopped fresh rosemary
½ tsp garlic salt
salt and freshly ground
    black pepper

Serves 4

Squeeze the lemon over the chicken, then rub the chicken skin with the olive oil, chopped rosemary and garlic salt and salt and pepper to taste. Stuff the chicken with the remaining lemon. Place the chicken directly on the low rack in the halogen oven. Cook at 225°C (440°F) for 45 minutes, turning it over every 15 minutes, then turn it down to 180°C (360°F) for the rest of the cooking time (about another 45 minutes) or until thoroughly cooked.

Rest in the halogen oven, turned off, for 10 minutes, before carving and serving.

NOW TRY THIS...

BACON-WRAPPED ROAST CHICKEN

Follow the recipe above, omitting the lemon. Before cooking, cover the chicken with strips of streaky bacon. The bacon will help baste the chicken and keep the flesh succulent. Cook as directed above, making sure to check that the chicken is cooked through and the juices run clear.

ROAST CHICKEN WITH LEMON, GARLIC AND TARRAGON

Follow the recipe as above, adding 1 tbsp chopped fresh tarragon to the garlic salt. Rub the mixture over the chicken, season with salt and freshly ground black pepper and cook as directed above.

SAFFRON AND LEMON CHICKEN

Mix together 1 tsp ground coriander, ½ tsp garlic salt, ¼ tsp ground ginger, ¼ tsp saffron threads and 2 tbsp olive oil. Follow the recipe as above, rubbing the saffron mixture over the chicken after squeezing over the lemon. Cook as directed above.

GARLIC BUTTER ROAST CHICKEN

Make 125 ml (4½ fl oz) garlic butter (page 112). Soften, then spread over the chicken. Sprinkle with 1 tbsp chopped fresh rosemary, and season with salt and freshly ground black pepper. Cook as directed above.

Stuffed Chicken Wrapped in Pancetta

A rich walnut and mushroom stuffing transforms chicken breasts into a wonderfully filling dish, ideal for a sophisticated dinner party or an everyday dinner.

4 chicken breasts
1 tbsp olive oil
100 g (4 oz) finely chopped
    mushrooms
1 shallot, finely chopped
1 clove garlic, crushed
25 g (1 oz) chopped walnuts
3 tbsp freshly chopped parsley
salt and ground black pepper
8 slices pancetta
olive oil to drizzle

Red Wine Sauce
1 tbsp olive oil
2 shallots, finely chopped
300 ml (10 fl oz) red wine
60 ml (2 fl oz) port
125 ml (4½ fl oz) good-quality
    chicken stock
2 tbsp redcurrant jelly
1 tbsp tomato purée
2 tsp cornflour mixed with
    2 tbsp water

Serves 4

With a sharp knife, cut a slit in the side of each chicken breast to make a pocket. Set aside.

In a medium frying pan, heat the oil over a low heat, then sauté the mushrooms, shallot and garlic until soft. Remove from the heat, and add the walnuts, parsley and salt and pepper. Leave to cool. Stuff the mixture into the chicken pockets, then wrap 2 slices of pancetta around each chicken breast to hold them together. Place the chicken breasts on a greased ovenproof dish and drizzle with a little olive oil and season with a little more salt and pepper. Place on the low rack of the halogen oven and turn the temperature to 200°C (400°F). Switch the timer to 35 minutes.

Turn the chicken over halfway through the cooking time.

While the chicken is cooking, make the red wine sauce. In a medium saucepan, heat the oil and fry the shallots for 5 minutes until softened. Add the red wine, port and stock, and simmer until the liquid has reduced by two-thirds. Add the redcurrant jelly and tomato purée and stir until dissolved. Add the cornflour mixed with a little water and bring back to the boil, stirring until thickened.

Serve the chicken with the red wine sauce.

NOW TRY THIS...

CHICKEN CORDON BLEU

Open out the chicken breasts. Place 1 slice ham and 1 slice low-fat cheddar cheese on each breast. Fold the chicken breasts over in half, so that the ham and cheese are enclosed inside. Dredge each breast in flour, before dipping it in beaten egg and covering in breadcrumbs. Place on a plate, cover and chill for at least an hour, or until required. Place the chicken on a greased oven tray, and cook at 190°C (375°F) on the low rack of the halogen oven for 20 minutes. Turn the chicken over, and cook for another 20 minutes, or until golden brown. Serve immediately.

Bourbon and Maple Chicken

The intense heat from the halogen lamp lends an amazing flavour to this dish, caramelising the sugar in the sauce and making it irresistible.

1 chicken, cut into 8 pieces,
   and skinned
160 ml (6 fl oz) red wine
4 tbsp soy sauce
2 tbsp red wine vinegar
1 tbsp tomato purée
2 tbsp maple syrup
2 tbsp bourbon
1 tsp ground ginger
1 tsp mustard powder
2 cloves garlic, crushed
watercress, to serve

Serves 4

Place the chicken on the round oven tray and cook on the high rack of the halogen oven at 220°C (425°F) for 15 minutes, turning the chicken over halfway through cooking time.

In a medium bowl, whisk together the red wine, soy sauce, vinegar, tomato purée, maple syrup, bourbon, ginger, mustard powder and garlic, until well combined. Spoon half the sauce over the chicken and cook for 5 minutes at 220°C (425°F). Then lower the heat to 190°C (375°F) and cook for another 5 minutes, then turn the chicken over and spoon on the remaining sauce. Cook for 5 minutes more, then transfer the chicken to a serving plate and keep warm in a low oven. Pour the sauce from the oven tray into a small saucepan, place over medium heat and bring to the boil. Simmer for 5–8 minutes, until the sauce has reduced in volume. Serve the chicken immediately, with the sauce poured on top, and garnished with watercress. This dish goes well with basmati rice with added chopped red pepper and a small finely chopped onion, and garnished with freshly chopped spring onions.

ANOTHER WAY

If you would rather not use alcohol in this dish, substitute good-quality chicken stock for the red wine and omit the bourbon.

Coconut Chicken with Sweet Chilli Dip

The coconut in this dish creates a wonderful, fragrant aroma – it is so exotic no one will guess it was cooked in a halogen oven!

8 skinless and boneless
    chicken thighs
1 tbsp lime juice
2 tsp garam masala
25 g (1 oz) flour
salt and freshly ground
    black pepper
25 g (1 oz) breadcrumbs
40 g (1½ oz) flaked coconut
1 egg, lightly beaten

sweet chilli sauce, to serve

Serves 4

Trim any visible fat from the chicken thighs and check for bits of bone. Cut each thigh in half. Place on a plate, sprinkle with the lime juice and garam masala and leave to marinate while you continue the preparation. Place the flour on a plate and season with salt and pepper. On another plate, mix the breadcrumbs and coconut. Put the egg on a third plate. Pat the chicken dry with kitchen paper, and roll each piece in the seasoned flour. Place in the beaten egg and then in the breadcrumb and coconut mix.

Find a heatproof sheet that will fit inside your halogen oven and spray it lightly with cooking oil. Place the breaded chicken on the sheet, and spray

ANOTHER WAY

For an easy variation on this dish, omit the lime juice and chilli sauce and use 1 tbsp Cajun seasoning (page 116), in the breadcrumbs.

lightly with the oil. Place the pan on the high rack, turn on the heat to 400°F, and switch the timer to 35 minutes. After about 15 minutes, turn the chicken over with tongs. Cook for the remaining 15–20 minutes, or until browned and crispy. Serve with the chili sauce.

Lemon Chicken

This is a wonderful Chinese dish to cook quickly on a busy weeknight.

2 chicken breasts, cubed
1 tbsp. soy sauce
2 tbsp. plum sauce
1 tbsp. lemon juice

For the Sauce
¼ tbsp cornstarch
2 tbsp. cold water
2 tbsp. rice vinegar
2 tbsp. plum sauce
½ tbsp. sugar
1 cup good-quality chicken stock
4 tbsp. lemon juice
½ lemon

In a large mixing bowl, combine the cubed chicken with the soy sauce, plum sauce, and lemon juice. Tip mixture onto the round oven tray and cook on the low rack in the halogen oven at 260°C (500°F) for 12 minutes. Stir, then cook for 3 minutes more.

Meanwhile, mix the cornflour with the cold water, then add the rice vinegar, plum sauce, sugar, chicken stock and lemon juice. Grate the zest from the half lemon into the mixture, then

ANOTHER WAY

This lemon sauce also makes an excellent accompaniment for white fish fillets.

slice the lemon and add to the sauce mixture. Mix the sauce and pour it over the chicken. Cook for a further 8 minutes at 200°C (400°F). Serve immediately with steamed rice.

Serves 4

Moroccan-Spiced Butterfly Quail

Quails are very small birds, so you need to serve one per person. You could substitute tiny chickens if you cannot find quails.

2 cloves garlic, crushed
1 tbsp ground cumin
1 tbsp ground coriander
1 tbsp ground cinnamon
1 tbsp paprika
salt and freshly ground
    black pepper
2 tbsp olive oil
4 quails, spatchcocked

Serves 4

Wash and pat dry the quails. In a small bowl, mix the garlic and spices together. Wipe olive oil and then pat on garlic and spice mixture all over each quail.

Place the birds on the oven tray, and cook on the low rack at 200°C (400°F) for 10 minutes each side, or until the birds are cooked through. Depending on the size of the birds, you may need to do this in batches, so keep them warm while you cook the rest of the birds. Serve immediately.

ANOTHER WAY

To butterfly or spatchcock a chicken or another bird, first turn the bird upside down and cut along one side of the backbone with kitchen shears or a sharp knife. Rotate the chicken around, and cut along the other side of the backbone, then cut it away. Open the bird up like a book, and find the diamond-shaped breastbone. Cut along both sides of the breastbone, run your fingers along either side and pull it out. You might need to cut it away from the breast meat underneath. Trim away any excess fat from either side of the bird, and it is ready to cook.

Duck Breasts with Redcurrant Sauce

The sweetness of the redcurrant sauce complements the stronger flavour of the duck breast. Serve with steamed vegetables and mashed potatoes.

1 onion, finely chopped
1 tsp olive oil
2 duck breasts
pinch salt
½ tbsp cornflour
2 tbsp cold water
1 chicken stock cube
300 ml (10 fl oz) boiling water
3 tbsp redcurrant jelly
½ tbsp brown sugar

Serves 2

Mix the chopped onion with the olive oil and place on the round baking tray. Score the skin of the duck breasts and rub with salt. Place ducks on top of the onion and cook at 230°C (450°F) in the halogen oven on the low rack for 15 minutes. Turn the duck breasts over and cook for 5 minutes more.

Mix the cornflour in the cold water. Dissolve the stock cube in the boiling water. Mix the dissolved cornflour, stock, redcurrant jelly and brown sugar to a smooth liquid.

Turn the duck breasts back over, cover with the sauce and cook for an additional 5 minutes. Turn off the oven and allow the duck to rest for 5 minutes, still in the oven. Remove and serve with the sauce.

TIP

The halogen oven is perfect for cooking meat in this way. Try using this method and sauce with lamb chops or steaks.

Lemon and Oregano Pork Escalopes

Pork coated in breadcrumbs and baked in the halogen oven stays moist inside and crunchy on the outside, and is delicious served with lemon or garlic mayonnaise.

550 g (1¼ lb) pork fillet,
    in 1 or 2 pieces
25 g (1 oz) flour
salt and freshly ground
    black pepper
2 eggs, beaten
finely grated zest of 1 lemon
100–150 g (4–6 oz) fresh
    breadcrumbs
2 tsp dried oregano
1 tsp sunflower oil
spray oil

Serves 4

Cut the pork into 8 slices, about 2.5 cm (1 in) thick, and place them between sheets of parchment paper. Beat with a kitchen mallet or a rolling pin until they are about 6 mm (¼ in) thick. Set out 3 plates. On the first, put the flour, seasoned with salt and pepper; on the second, put the beaten egg; and on the third, mix together the lemon zest, breadcrumbs and oregano. Dip each pork escalope first in the flour, then into the egg and finally roll in the breadcrumbs, until well coated.

Lightly grease the oven tray with sunflower oil, and add 4 escalopes at a time. Cook at 200°C

ANOTHER WAY

To make garlic or lemon mayonnaise, just add 1 crushed clove of garlic or 1 tsp lemon zest to 5 tbsp mayonnaise.

(400°F) on the high rack of the halogen oven for 5 minutes, turn the escalopes over, spray with a little oil and cook for another 5 minutes, until the breadcrumbs are crisp and the pork is cooked. Keep warm while you cook all the escalopes. Serve with either garlic or lemon mayonnaise.

Slow Roasted Belly of Pork

This cut of meat needs lots of time and little attention. It is best when cooked slowly, for at least 5 hours. The skin should crisp to form crackling and the fat should melt away.

1 kg (2 lb 4 oz) belly pork
4 sprigs fresh rosemary
2 sprigs fresh thyme
1 tsp chopped dried
    bay leaves
3 cloves garlic, halved
freshly ground
    black pepper
1 tbsp salt, for rubbing
    the meat

Serves 4

Ask the butcher to score the skin, if it has not been done already. If you have to do it yourself, use a very sharp craft knife or box cutter.

Place the pork, skin-side down, on the oven tray. Distribute the rosemary, thyme, bay leaves and garlic evenly over the meat of the belly. Season with plenty of pepper. Press a sheet of aluminium foil over the belly flesh to make sure the garlic and herbs will not move. Turn the whole lot over, so the skin side is up, and form the foil into a snug cocoon around the pork, leaving the skin exposed and ensuring that the meat is completely enclosed. Rub the surface with the salt.

ANOTHER WAY

If you like crackling, after cooking turn the heat back up to 230°C (450°F) and cook 5 minutes more.

Cook on the low rack of the halogen oven for 5 minutes at 230°C (450°F). Turn the heat down to 120°C (250°F), leave the pork on the low rack and cook for a further 5 hours. Let the pork rest for 15 minutes before serving.

83

Greek-Style Roast Lamb

This wonderful, hearty dish of lamb, tomatoes and olives is full of Mediterranean flavours. It is best served with rice and salad.

1 red onion, sliced
1 tbsp oil
1 (1 kg/2 lb) leg of lamb
2 sprigs fresh rosemary
5 cloves garlic, sliced
salt and freshly ground black pepper
400 g (13 oz) tinned tomatoes
2 tbsp chopped olives (use your
   favourite variety)
1 tsp dried oregano
2 tbsp white wine vinegar
1 tsp sugar
3 tbsp water

Serves 4

Place the sliced onion on a greased round baking tray. Make narrow cuts into the lamb on all sides. Stud the lamb with the rosemary and garlic, season with salt and pepper and place it on top of the onions. Cook on the low rack of the halogen oven at 240°C (460°F) for 15 minutes. Turn the lamb over and cook for an additional 15 minutes.

Mix the tomatoes, olives, dried oregano, vinegar, sugar and water together.

Lift up the lamb and place this tomato mixture underneath. Lower the oven temperature to 175°C (350°F) and cook the lamb on the low rack for a further 40 minutes for rare lamb. Cook for an additional 40 minutes for well-done lamb.

Turn off the oven and allow lamb to rest in the oven for a further 10 minutes, then serve with the sauce.

ANOTHER WAY

If you like a sweeter sauce for the lamb, add 1 tbsp of honey with the tomatoes.

Lamb Brochettes with Basil and Oregano

Lean lamb, rolled in basil and oregano, is threaded onto skewers with red pepper and grilled until slightly charred on the edges but still slightly pink in the centre.

550 g (1 lb 4 oz) lean lamb,
  from the leg
1 tbsp dried basil
1 tbsp dried oregano
1 large red pepper, deseeded,
  cut into 2.5 cm (1in) pieces
2 tbsp olive oil
salt and freshly ground
  black pepper
Béarnaise sauce, to serve

Serves 4

If using wooden skewers, soak for 30 minutes in cold water. Cut the lamb into 2.5 cm (1 in) cubes. On a plate, mix together the basil and oregano. Roll the lamb cubes in the herbs. Thread the lamb, alternating with the pepper pieces, onto 6–8 skewers. Do not pack them too close together; leave a bit of a gap. Place on a plate and drizzle with the olive oil. Leave covered in the refrigerator to marinate for at least 30 minutes, or longer if you have time. Transfer the skewers to the oven tray, season with a little salt and plenty of pepper and grill at 200°C (400°F) on the high rack of the halogen oven for 4–5 minutes. Turn over and grill for another 4–5 minutes, or until

ANOTHER WAY

Newly picked herbs add a delightful freshness to the taste of any dish. Try fresh thyme and rosemary instead of dried basil and oregano, and red onion in place of red pepper. Vary the vegetables according to season, preference and availability.

slightly chargrilled on the edges but still a little pink in the centre. Serve immediately, with your favourite Béarnaise sauce.

Lamb Steaks with Herb Crust

The crunchiness of the breadcrumb coating works well with the texture of the lamb. These steaks are great with mashed potatoes and a tossed salad.

4 lamb steaks (2.5 cm/1 in
  thick)
2 tbsp honey
1 tsp Dijon mustard
25 g (1 oz) white breadcrumbs
2 tsp freshly chopped parsley
salt and freshly ground
  black pepper
1 tbsp olive oil, plus a little for
  greasing pan

Serves 4

Place the lamb steaks on the round baking tray and cook on the high rack in the halogen oven at 260°C (500°F) for 4 minutes per side. Remove steaks and let them drain on paper towels.

Mix together the honey and mustard in a bowl. In a separate bowl, combine the breadcrumbs, parsley, salt, pepper and 1 tbsp olive oil. Wipe the remaining oil on the clean round oven tray.

Brush the honey mustard on both sides of each lamb steak, then dredge each steak in the crumb mixture until evenly coated. Place the steaks on

ANOTHER WAY

Add 1/2 tsp. dried oregano to the breadcrumb coating or try other types of mustard, such as wholegrain or yellow mustard.

the greased oven tray and cook on the low rack of the halogen oven at 175°C (350°F) for 3–5 minutes per side, or until they are done to your preference. Serve immediately.

Rack of Lamb with Rosemary and Garlic

Rosemary and garlic are perfect partners for this succulent roast lamb, cooked to perfection.

1 (1 kg/2 lb) rack of lamb
2 sprigs fresh rosemary
1 whole garlic bulb (top
    cut off)
olive oil

Redcurrant Sauce
1 tbsp olive oil
2 shallots, finely diced
400 g (14 oz) redcurrants
125 ml (4 fl oz) red wine
125 ml (4 fl oz) chicken stock

Serves 4

Place the lamb on the low rack in the halogen oven and cover with the rosemary. Place the garlic on its stalk next to the leg, drizzle everything with olive oil and cook at 240°C (460°F) for 10 minutes. Turn the lamb over, reduce the temperature to 175°C (350°F) and cook for 20 minutes. Turn again and cook for a further 20 minutes for pink, 25 minutes for medium or 30–35 minutes for well done. Remove the lamb from the oven and leave to rest in a warm place for a few minutes before serving.

To make the sauce, fry the shallots in a small frying pan with a little olive oil until translucent, then add the redcurrants. Cook until they burst, then add the red wine and chicken stock. Increase the heat and reduce the sauce by about half, then strain into a small serving dish.

Serve the lamb with the warm redcurrant sauce, with peas and mashed potatoes.

ANOTHER WAY

With any kind of roast meat, resting is essential. Think of the resting time as part of the cooking time and plan accordingly. It can actually be helpful to have a few minutes to assemble the other components of the meal.

Filet Mignon with a Trio of Sauces

Steak can be served with a choice of sauces or plain if you prefer. We have chosen three of our favourite sauces – pepper sauce, blue cheese sauce and herb butter.

1 fillet steak
1 tbsp oil
salt and freshly ground
    black pepper

Pepper Sauce
¼ tsp crushed or coarsely
    ground black peppercorns
125 ml (4 fl oz) double cream
2 tbsp steak sauce
pinch salt

Blue Cheese Sauce
2 tbsp blue cheese, crumbled
125 ml (4 fl oz) double cream
pinch freshly ground
    black pepper

Herb Butter
2 tbsp butter, softened
2 tbsp freshly chopped parsley

Serves 1

Brush the steak with the oil and season to taste with salt and pepper. Place on the round baking tray, set it on the high rack of the halogen oven and cook at 260°C (500°F) for 5 minutes on each side (or to your taste). While the steak is cooking, prepare the sauce you're using.

Pepper Sauce

Mix together all the ingredients, and pour over the cooked steak. Cook for a further 5 minutes at 260°C (500°F).

Blue Cheese Sauce

Break the blue cheese into pieces, then mix with the cream, season with pepper, pour over cooked steak and cook for a further 5 minutes at 260°C (500°F).

Herb Butter

Mix the butter and parsley together. Check the steak is done and place a dollop of the butter on top when ready to serve.

ANOTHER WAY

To make a delicious Cajun seasoning for steak, mix together
½ tsp ground sea salt
1 tbsp paprika
1 tbsp cayenne pepper
½ tsp garlic salt
½ tbsp freshly ground black
    pepper
½ tbsp ground white pepper
½ tsp ground mustard
¼ tsp pumpkin pie spice
1 tsp dried basil
Place the steak in a large bowl with 1 small red onion, sliced, ½ tbsp vegetable oil and 1 tbsp Cajun seasoning. Mix well. Allow to marinate for at least 10 minutes or overnight. Place the marinated steak with the onions on a round oven tray, and cook on the high rack at 250°C (480°F) for:
• Rare: 5 minutes on each side
• Medium: 7 minutes each side
• Well done: 10 minutes on each side.

Rib Roast with Red Wine Gravy

A rib roast works so well in the halogen oven. The radiant heat seals the outside and makes it succulent and juicy on the inside. No need to pan-fry first!

1 (1 kg/2 lb) rib roast (2 ribs)
1 tbsp butter
salt and finely ground
    black pepper
4 cloves garlic, sliced
125 ml (4 fl oz) red wine
1–2 beef stock cubes mixed
    with 400 ml (1 pt) boiling
    water
1 tsp sugar
1 tsp dried Italian mixed herbs
1 onion, finely chopped
1 tbsp cornflour

Serves 4

Rub the beef with the butter and sprinkle with salt and pepper. Pierce the beef all over and stud with the pieces of sliced garlic.

Pour the red wine and beef stock into the base/glass bowl of the halogen oven. Stir in the sugar, mixed herbs and onions.

Place the beef directly on the low rack in the halogen oven and cook at 240°C (460°F) for 20 minutes, turning every 10 minutes. Then lower the heat to 175°C (350°F) and cook for an additional 30 minutes, turning every 10 minutes. If you want rare meat, remove the roast from the oven. For medium doneness, continue cooking the beef for 20 minutes more, or 35 minutes for well-done meat.

Let the beef rest. Remove the low rack from the halogen oven. Mix a little water with the cornflour, then stir into the red wine mixture in the base of the halogen oven. Cook for 5 minutes at 260°C (500°F) to make a gravy. Add the beef to the gravy, turn off the heat, close the lid of the halogen oven and let the meat rest, in the oven, for 10 minutes, before serving.

ANOTHER WAY

If you don't want to use wine, replace it with beef stock.

Thai Fishcakes

These spicy and flavourful little fishcakes are wonderful as a starter or as a main course. Serve with sweet chilli sauce for dipping.

1 tsp vegetable oil, for greasing
500 g (1 lb 2 oz) white
    fish fillet(s)
1 egg, lightly beaten
2 tbsp cornflour
1 tbsp fish sauce
1–2 tsp red Thai curry paste
1 tsp deseeded and finely
    chopped red chilli
2 tbsp freshly chopped coriander
salt and freshly ground
    black pepper
2 spring onions, chopped
sweet chilli sauce, to serve

Makes 8–9

Lightly brush the oven tray with vegetable oil. Chop the fish into 1 cm (½ in) pieces, and place into a food processor. Pulse until coarsely chopped. Add egg, cornflour, fish sauce, curry paste, chilli and coriander, and season with salt and pepper. Pulse a few times until combined. Mix in the onions. Using your hands, form into small fishcakes about 7.5 cm (3 in) in diameter. Place them on the oiled oven tray, set it on the high rack of the halogen oven and cook at 225°C (440°F) for 5 minutes per side, or until lightly browned and cooked through. Keep warm while you cook all the fishcakes. Serve with sweet chilli sauce.

TIP

Make your own red Thai curry paste by processing 2 shallots, 2 cloves garlic, 2 red chillies, 2.5 cm (1 in) piece root ginger, 1 tbsp fish or soy sauce, 1 tsp each ground coriander and cumin, 1 chopped lemongrass stalk, zest and juice of 1 lime and salt and freshly ground black pepper. Cover and store any surplus in the refrigerator for up to 1 week, or freeze for up to 1 month.

Tilapia with Parmesan Crust

In the halogen oven this topping becomes a lovely crispy crust that helps to keep the fish really succulent while complementing the flavour of the fish.

4 tbsp fresh breadcrumbs
2 tbsp freshly grated Parmesan
    cheese
½ tbsp chopped fresh oregano
½ tbsp chopped fresh parsley
2 tbsp olive oil, plus a little more
    for greasing
1 tbsp freshly squeezed lime juice
2 (200 g/8 oz) tilapia fillets

Serves 2

Mix the breadcrumbs, Parmesan, oregano and parsley together in a bowl. Stir in the oil and lime juice to make a paste.

Lightly rub a round baking dish with the remaining oil. Place the tilapia fillets in the dish. Spread the paste on top of the fillets, covering them evenly. Place the dish in the halogen oven on the low rack and cook at 225°C (440°F) for 12 minutes, or until the fillets are thoroughly cooked. Serve immediately, with a green salad.

ANOTHER WAY

This is an easy dish to vary. You can use other white fish fillets such as cod or sea bass. Also, try other herbs, such as thyme, dill or chives.

Haddock and Cheese Ramekins

This dish is even better when half the haddock is smoked. However, you can use fresh haddock if you can't find smoked haddock.

vegetable oil, for greasing
350 g (12 oz) fresh haddock
    fillet (or 175 g/6 oz fresh
    and 175 g/6 oz smoked)
250 ml (8 fl oz) water
4 tbsp dry white wine
1 fish stock cube
6 peppercorns
1 bay leaf
1 shallot, finely sliced
50 g (2 oz) butter
150 g (6 oz) sliced mushrooms
2 tbsp flour
freshly ground black pepper
50 g (2 oz) finely grated
    cheddar cheese
25 g (1 oz) fresh breadcrumbs

Serves 4

Grease 6 ramekins (10 cm/4 in diameter) with a little vegetable oil.

In a large saucepan, place the fish with the water and wine. Add the fish stock cube, peppercorns, bay leaf and shallot, and bring to the boil. Cover and poach gently for about 12 minutes.

Strain off the liquid and reserve. Flake the fish, discarding the skin and any bones. Discard also the peppercorns, bay leaf and shallot. In a medium saucepan over medium heat, melt the butter, add the mushrooms and sauté for 5 minutes. Stir in the flour and cook gently for 2 minutes, stirring continuously. Lower the heat slightly, and gradually add the strained cooking liquid. Bring to the boil and continue to cook, stirring, until the sauce thickens. If it thickens too much, add a little water or white wine. Add half the cheese, and season to taste with salt and pepper, stirring until the cheese has melted. Gently fold in the fish, spoon the mixture into the prepared ramekins and top with the remaining cheese and crumbs. Place 3 on the oven tray on the low rack of the halogen oven at 175°C (350°F). Cook for about 8 minutes, or until golden brown and nice and hot. Keep warm while you cook the other 3. Serve immediately.

ANOTHER WAY

This dish can be made with any available firm-fleshed white fish. You could also try using a mixture of salmon and shrimp, and adding a little freshly chopped parsley to the sauce.

Pesto-Crusted Cod

The intense heat of the halogen oven helps to cook the fish very quickly while keeping it from becoming dry and tough. You can use any white fish in place of the cod fillets.

2 cod fillets

Pesto
2 cloves garlic
2 tbsp grated Parmesan cheese
2 tbsp pine nuts
salt and freshly ground
    black pepper
2 large handfuls fresh basil
4 tbsp olive oil, plus a little
    extra for greasing

Serves 2

To make the pesto, chop the garlic with the Parmesan in a food processor. Add the pine nuts and the salt and pepper to taste, and process. Add the basil leaves and oil, and process to your desired consistency.

Lightly grease a round baking dish. Place the cod fillets in the dish and spread the pesto on top of the fish. Place in the halogen oven on the low rack and cook at 225°C (440°F) for 12 minutes or until the fillets are thoroughly cooked. Serve with a green salad.

ANOTHER WAY

The pesto will keep up to 3 days in a sealed container. It is also great with cooked penne pasta.

Grilled Sole and Lemon

Fish cooks so well in the halogen oven. The quick heating up of the oven cooks it quickly, but seals in the juices, keeping the fish from drying out. This recipe is good with boiled new potatoes and steamed sugarsnap peas or another green vegetable.

2 medium-sized sole fillets
    (or flounder)
1 tbsp butter, softened
salt and freshly ground
    black pepper
1 lemon, cut into 6 wedges
1 tbsp freshly chopped parsley

Serves 2

Rub sole fillets with butter and season with salt and pepper. Place them on the round baking tray. Arrange the lemon wedges around the fillets.

Place the tray on the low rack of the halogen oven and cook at 200°C (400°F) for 15 minutes, turning over halfway through. Serve the fillets with the lemon, sprinkled with chopped parsley.

ANOTHER WAY

Five minutes before the end of cooking, brush a spoonful of red or green pesto over the fish.

Butter-Roasted Monkfish

Monkfish is a firm, meaty white fish that is simply delicious when roasted in a hot halogen oven. This will be a family favourite in no time at all.

250 g (10 oz) monkfish, cubed
1 tbsp sweet chilli sauce
¼ tsp mixed dried Italian herbs
pinch salt and pepper
1 tbsp melted butter
juice of 1 lime
1 large onion, cut into 2.5 cm (1 in) squares
1 red pepper, cut into 2.5 cm (1 in) squares
12 cherry tomatoes
120 g (5 oz) fresh spinach leaves

Serves 4

Place the cubed monkfish in a bowl and add sweet chilli sauce, mixed dried herbs, salt and pepper, butter and half the lime juice. Mix and leave to marinate for 10 minutes, then place on the round oven tray with the onion, red pepper and cherry tomatoes. Place on the high rack at 225°C (440°F) for 8 minutes. Take out and place in a bowl.

Place the spinach on the round oven tray and place the monkfish, peppers, onion and cherry tomatoes on top. Cook for a further 4 minutes at 225°C (440°F) or until cooked. Use the rest of the juice of the lime on the monkish and serve on a bed of salad.

NOW TRY THIS...

TUNA AND SESAME SEED SALAD

Follow the recipe above, substituting 250 g (10 oz) diced tuna steak for the monkfish. Cook as directed. Sprinkle the tuna with toasted sesame seeds before serving on a bed of salad.

SEAFOOD MEDLEY

Cook as directed above, substituting 250 g (10 oz) mixed scallops and shrimp for half the monkfish.

SPICY MONKFISH

Follow the recipe above, adding ½ tsp ground cumin and ½ tsp dried red chilli flakes along with the mixed herbs. Cook as directed above.

MOROCCAN MONKFISH

Follow the recipe above, adding ½ tsp ground cumin along with the mixed herbs. Cook as directed above. Serve with couscous.

Salmon and Green Pepper Sauté

Fish, bacon and green peppers with tomatoes and cheese make an interesting combination for dinner, sure to be enjoyed by children and adults alike.

1 tbsp vegetable oil, plus extra
   for greasing
700 g (1½ lb) oily fish fillets,
   such as salmon
25 g (1 oz) flour
salt and freshly ground
   black pepper
4 strips bacon, chopped
½ green pepper, sliced
3 tomatoes, skinned
   and quartered
50 g (2 oz) grated
   cheddar cheese

Serves 4

Grease a baking dish that will fit in your halogen oven with a little vegetable oil.

Cut the salmon fillet into pieces, each about 5 cm (2 in). Season the flour with salt and pepper. Toss the salmon in the seasoned flour.

Cook the bacon and green pepper together in the halogen oven on the oven tray on the high rack at 215°C (420°F) for 5 minutes, stirring halfway through. Transfer to the baking dish. Add the fish to the oven tray and drizzle with a little vegetable oil. Cook in the halogen oven for 3 minutes on each side, taking care not to break it up. Transfer the fish to the baking dish, add the tomatoes and season to taste with salt and pepper. Sprinkle the cheese on top, and return the baking dish to the oven to cook on the high rack at 175°C (350°F) for a further 5 minutes, or until heated through. Serve immediately.

ANOTHER WAY

Replace the salmon with any firm-fleshed white fish. An excellent choice would be a combination of salmon, cod and shrimp.

Roasted Mediterranean Vegetables

The halogen oven is perfect for roasting these vegetables, as they char beautifully on the edges, hold their shape well and remain succulent and full of flavour.

1 small aubergine, cubed
1 courgette, quartered lengthways
    and sliced
1 red pepper, deseeded and cut into
    1 cm (½ in) pieces
1 small red onion, peeled and cut
    into wedges
1 tbsp olive oil
salt and freshly ground black pepper
6–8 cherry tomatoes
2 tbsp freshly chopped basil leaves

Serves 4

Lightly grease the oven tray, and add the aubergine, courgette, pepper and onion pieces. Drizzle with the olive oil, season with salt and pepper and place on the low rack of the halogen oven. Cook for 10 minutes at 200°C (400°F). Turn the vegetables over, add the tomatoes and cook for 5–10 minutes more, or until the vegetables are lightly charred on the edges and tender. Just before serving, sprinkle with freshly chopped basil.

ANOTHER WAY
If you have two dishes to cook, and only one oven, you can prepare this dish up to the last 5 minutes. It will heat up quickly, while you are serving another dish.

Aubergine Parmigiana

This wonderful Italian dish is a good example of how you can create a meal in one dish with the halogen oven, whereas the conventional way would use many pans.

1 medium aubergine, sliced
4 tbsp olive oil
½ onion, chopped
1 clove garlic, chopped
400 g (14 oz) tinned chopped
    tomatoes in juice
4 tbsp tomato ketchup
1 tsp mixed dried Italian herbs
salt and freshly ground
    black pepper
50 g (2 oz) freshly grated
    Parmesan cheese
1 handful fresh oregano (optional)

Serves 4

Place the aubergine slices on the round oven tray, brush with a little oil and cook on the low rack in the halogen oven at 260°C (500°F) for 6 minutes on each side. Remove and set aside.

In an ovenproof baking dish, cook the onion with 1 tbsp olive oil for 3 minutes at 260°C (500°F) on the low rack. Add the garlic and ½ tbsp olive oil, cook for 1 minute, then add the tomatoes, ketchup, mixed herbs and season to taste. Cook for 5 minutes. Remove from the oven, stir and pour half the sauce into a bowl.

Layer aubergine slices on top of the sauce remaining in the baking dish. Cover with some

ANOTHER WAY
Add 25 g (1 oz) chopped chorizo to the tomato sauce for extra depth of flavour and spice.

Parmesan and some of the tomato sauce, then repeat this process. Finish with the remaining Parmesan and cook on the low rack at 175°C (350°F) for 20 minutes. Remove from the oven, cut into slices and serve immediately with a sprinkling of fresh oregano.

Potato Dauphinoise with Swiss Cheese

This is a rich, creamy and tasty dish, well suited to special occasions. It is included here to show that you can cook potato casseroles in the halogen oven, although it is necessary to parboil the potatoes first.

1 kg (2 lb) potatoes
2 tbsp butter, softened, plus extra for greasing
1 medium onion, finely chopped
150 g (6 oz) finely grated Gruyère cheese
salt and freshly ground black pepper
160 ml (6 fl oz) plus 2 tbsp single cream

Serves 4–5

Grease a shallow baking dish that will fit inside your halogen oven.

Peel the potatoes, leave them whole and parboil them for 10 minutes in a large saucepan filled with boiling water. Drain and leave to cool for 10 minutes. Slice the potatoes as thinly as possible without letting them fall apart. Put a layer of potato slices, overlapping, in the bottom of the dish. Dot with butter, sprinkle with some of the onion and cheese and season with salt and pepper. Pour in about a quarter of the single cream. Continue with these layers until all the ingredients have been used up, finishing with a layer of cheese and pouring the remaining cream over the top.

Cover with a lid or buttered foil, and bake on the low rack of the halogen oven at 200°C (400°F) for 50 minutes, or until the potatoes are tender when pierced with a skewer. Remove the lid or foil, turn the heat up to 220°C (425°F) and cook until the top layer of cheese is bubbling. Watch closely; this may only take 2 or 3 minutes.

ANOTHER WAY

For a less expensive, less rich dish, substitute cheddar cheese and milk for the Gruyère and cream. You could also add garlic and parsley to the layers if you wish.

Roasted Potatoes with Rosemary

Potatoes roasted in the halogen oven are crispy on the outside and light and fluffy on the inside. Why not try different variations by adding spices, herbs and oils?

6 large potatoes, peeled
    and quartered
125 ml (4 fl oz) melted duck fat,
    lard or vegetable fat
½ tsp sea salt
pinch white pepper
1 sprig fresh rosemary

Serves 4

In a medium saucepan half-filled with boiling water, cook the potatoes for 10 minutes. Drain, replace the potatoes in the pan, pour in the melted fat and season with salt and pepper. Cover the pan and shake to roughen the edges of the potatoes.

Place the potatoes on the round oven tray on the low rack of the halogen oven and cook at 260°C (500°F) for 20 minutes. Turn over the potatoes, sprinkle with the fresh rosemary leaves and cook for an additional 25 minutes. Remove and serve immediately.

ANOTHER WAY

This is good with sweet potatoes too, either alone or mixed with the white potatoes. Sweet potatoes will take less time to cook: cook for 15 minutes at 260°C (500°F), then turn and cook for 20 minutes more.

Honey Parsnips

The halogen oven really helps to caramelise the honey and sweeten up the parsnips. These are great served with roast meats.

4 parsnips, peeled
    and quartered
2 tbsp olive oil
salt and freshly ground
    black pepper
3 tbsp honey

Serves 4

Place the parsnips, olive oil, salt and pepper in a large bowl and mix together. Tip onto the round oven baking tray. Place on the lower rack in the halogen oven at 260°C (500°F) and cook, stirring every 5 minutes, for 15 minutes.

Drizzle with the honey, stir and cook for an additional 10 minutes. Serve hot.

ANOTHER WAY

To add a little something extra, garnish before serving with toasted sesame seeds.

Grilled Asparagus Wrapped in Parma Ham

Asparagus spears are so tasty wrapped with the Parma ham, and this makes a great dipping food.

16 asparagus spears
16 slices Parma ham
pinch salt and pepper
1 tbsp vegetable oil
½ tbsp fresh parsley, chopped

Dipping Sauce
2 tbsp sweet chilli sauce
4 tbsp cream cheese
2 tbsp mayonnaise

Put the asparagus in a suitably sized bowl and pour boiling water over the spears. Leave for 5 minutes.

Remove the asparagus from the water and wrap each spear in a slice of Parma ham. Place on a round oven tray, season and drizzle with oil. Grill the wrapped asparagus on high rack at 235°C (460°F) for 4 minutes.

ANOTHER WAY

This dip also makes the perfect accompaniment for tortilla chips.

For the dipping sauce, mix the sweet chilli sauce, cream cheese and mayonnaise together and serve.

Serves 4

Creamy Spinach Casserole

The creaminess of the cheese goes beautifully with the wilted spinach, making this a quick and easy dish to prepare and a great way to get kids to eat spinach.

200 g (8 oz) baby spinach
2 tbsp olive oil
¼ tsp garlic salt
250 g (10 oz) cream cheese
3 tbsp milk
½ tsp dried mixed Italian herbs

Combine the spinach, oil and garlic salt in a baking dish. Cook in the halogen oven on the low rack at 260°C (500°F) for 3 minutes.

Mix the cream cheese and milk together. Stir into the spinach and the Italian herbs and cook for 5 minutes, still at 260°C (500°F). Serve hot.

ANOTHER WAY

Add some crispy bacon sprinkles for added flavour. This also makes a great appetiser with crusty bread.

Serves 4

Quick Dinner Rolls

Nothing could be nicer than smelling freshly baked bread, especially when you have guests. This easy recipe is ideal for dinner parties, but it's so easy you can make it for a simple family dinner.

2 tsp fresh yeast or 1 tsp
   dried yeast
160 ml (6 fl oz) warm milk
   (45°C/110°F)
1 tsp sugar
200 g (8 oz) plain or bread
   flour, plus extra for
   kneading
½ tsp salt
60 ml (1½ fl oz) melted butter,
   plus more for greasing

Optional Flavourings
1 tsp chopped garlic
2 tsp chopped olives (Kalamata
   preferred)
3 tsp chopped sundried
   tomatoes

Makes 8

Mix the yeast with the milk and sugar. Leave for 6 minutes to dissolve.

Place the flour and salt in a large mixing bowl and mix in the melted butter. Add the yeast liquid and mix to a soft dough. Knead the dough on a lightly floured counter for 7 minutes, or until it becomes firm and elastic. To save time, you can use a freestanding mixer with a dough hook.

Let the dough rise in the mixing bowl, covered with a clean damp cloth. Leave in a warm place for 10 minutes, so the dough will expand. Knead the dough again for 2 minutes to reduce it to its original size. Now you can add your chosen flavouring to the dough, kneading to combine thoroughly. Shape into small rolls and place on a greased round oven tray.

Cook rolls in the halogen oven on the low rack at 225°C (440°F) for 15–25 minutes until cooked. The cooking time will vary depending on what size rolls you make. Leave to cool before serving.

TIP

Flavoured butter goes perfectly with these rolls. To make garlic butter, take 100 g (4 oz) unsalted butter, and melt slightly. Finely chop 3 cloves garlic and mix into the butter. You can also add other chopped herbs – try 1 tsp dried oregano or 2 tsp chopped fresh parsley. Place the garlic butter on a sheet of baking parchment, roll into a cylinder and refrigerate until needed.

SNACKS & DESSERTS

Potato Skins with Bacon and Cheese

A filling dish that makes a great snack or starter.

4 medium baking potatoes
4 strips bacon
1 small onion, finely chopped
2 tbsp mayonnaise
2 tsp cream cheese
salt and freshly ground
    black pepper
50 g (2 oz) cheddar cheese, grated

Serves 4

Wash and dry the potatoes, and place them on the low rack in the halogen oven. Cook at 260°C (500°F) for 45–60 minutes, turning every 15 minutes or until thoroughly cooked. Remove and slice in half lengthways. Set aside to cool.

Place the bacon on the round oven tray and cook on the low rack at 230°C (450°F) for 4 minutes per side. When cooked and crisp, chop the bacon.

With a small spoon, scoop out some of the potato, leaving the skins intact. Mix the potato in a bowl with the bacon, onion, mayonnaise, cream cheese and salt and pepper. Fill the skins with the mixture. Sprinkle with cheese.

When ready to serve, cook the potatoes on the high rack at 260°C (500°F) for 5 minutes or until hot and golden brown.

ANOTHER WAY

These can be made in advance but will need 10 minutes' more cooking time and will need to be cooked on the low rack of the halogen oven.

Crispy Potato Fries

Potato fries cooked in the halogen oven are so good — crispy on the outside and fluffy on the inside. The addition of Cajun seasoning adds depth to the flavour and a touch of spiciness.

Cajun Seasoning
½ tsp white pepper
½ tsp garlic powder
½ tsp onion powder
½ tsp ground red pepper
½ tsp paprika
½ tsp black pepper

4 medium potatoes, peeled, sliced
    and cut into thick strips
1 tbsp vegetable oil
salt and freshly ground
    black pepper

Serves 4

Make the Cajun seasoning by combining the ingredients in a small bowl.

In a large bowl, place the potatoes, add the oil and sprinkle on the Cajun seasoning. Add a little salt and plenty of freshly ground black pepper, and stir with a wooden spoon to coat the potatoes completely. Transfer to the round oven tray and bake, stirring occasionally, on the low rack of the halogen oven at 260°C (500°F) for 25 minutes, or until browned and crispy.

ANOTHER WAY

Vary the seasonings on the fries, using black mustard seeds or crushed cardamom seeds instead of Cajun spice. Or sprinkle with fresh herbs at the end of the cooking time. You could even sprinkle with a little finely grated cheddar cheese.

Spicy Potato Wedges with Sour Cream Dip

Nothing could be nicer than sitting down to watch a film with these wedges and a sour cream dip. These are also delicious with ketchup, ranch dressing or garlic mayonnaise.

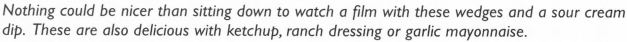

2 medium potatoes, cut
    into wedges
1 tbsp mayonnaise
1 tbsp sweet chilli sauce
3 tbsp olive oil
1 tbsp cayenne pepper, or to taste
pinch garlic salt
salt and freshly ground
    black pepper
125 ml (4 fl oz) sour cream
2 tbsp minced fresh chives

Serves 2

Place the potato wedges in a large mixing bowl. Combine the mayonnaise, sweet chilli sauce and olive oil with the seasonings, then mix well with the potatoes. Place the seasoned wedges on the round oven tray, and set the tray on the low rack in the halogen oven. Cook at 260°C (500°F) for 25 minutes, stirring occasionally, or until tender and golden brown.

While the potatoes are cooking, mix the sour cream with the chives. Keep chilled in a small

TIP

You can peel and cut the potatoes in advance, but they must be kept in water to prevent browning.

serving bowl until ready to serve. Serve the wedges immediately while hot with the sour cream dip.

Nachos with Salsa

A treat for when you sit around with friends watching a movie. You can substitute any favourite cheese if you want. This is good with sour cream and chive dip (page 114) or guacamole (page 44).

Salsa
2 ripe tomatoes, chopped
    and deseeded
2 spring onions, sliced
2 tbsp olive oil
1 tbsp lime juice
1 sliced jalapeño pepper
1 tbsp chopped coriander
salt and freshly ground
    black pepper

Nachos
1 bag favourite tortilla chips
100 g (4 oz) grated
    cheddar cheese

Serves 4

In a medium bowl, combine the salsa ingredients, check the seasoning and add more salt and pepper as needed. Leave to stand a while to meld the flavours together.

Pour the bag of chips into an ovenproof dish, spoon the salsa over the top, then sprinkle with the grated cheese. Cook in the halogen oven on the low rack at 200°C (400°F) for 8 minutes. Remove and serve immediately.

NOW TRY THIS...

VEGETABLE FEAST NACHOS

In a frying pan, fry 1 small courgette, diced, and ½ small red pepper, sliced. Add to the salsa ingredients listed above, along with 1 small tin sweetcorn. Cook as above.

SPICY NACHOS

Follow the recipe as above, adding 1 tsp hot sauce, such as Tabasco, to the salsa. Spoon the salsa over the chips, then sprinkle over 50 g (2 oz) diced chorizo, before adding the cheese. Cook as above.

MUSHROOM NACHOS WITH REFRIED BEANS

Place 75 g (3 oz) sliced portobello mushrooms in a small frying pan, with 1 tsp olive oil, 1 tbsp soy sauce and 1 tsp lemon juice. Fry gently until the mushrooms are soft.

Drain. Follow the recipe as directed above, but spoon 100g (4 oz) refried beans over the chips before adding the salsa. Next add the cooked mushrooms and the shredded cheese. Cook as above.

GREEK NACHOS

Follow the recipe, adding 25 g (1 oz) sliced black or green olives, and omitting the lime juice and jalapeño. Substitute feta cheese for the cheddar cheese. Cook as directed above.

Tomato Bruschetta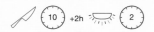

Chopped tomatoes with a touch of garlic and a little chopped basil spooned onto crispy garlic bread make a fresh and healthy accompaniment to a breakfast or brunch buffet. This is a great way to use up day-old French bread.

300 g (10 oz) chopped tomatoes
3 tbsp finely chopped red onion
1 large clove garlic, crushed or
finely chopped
2 tbsp freshly chopped basil
4 tbsp extra-virgin olive oil
½ tsp red wine vinegar
salt and freshly ground
black pepper
1 tsp garlic salt
½ baguette, cut diagonally into
15 cm (6 in) slices

Makes 6 slices

In a large bowl, mix together the tomatoes, onion, garlic, basil, 2 tsp olive oil and the red wine vinegar. Season with a little salt and pepper, cover and chill in the refrigerator for about 2 hours.

In a small bowl, mix the remaining olive oil with the garlic salt and brush it over both sides of each slice of bread. Toast the bread on the high rack of the halogen oven at 220°C (425°F) for 1–2 minutes per side, until nicely browned. Remove from the oven and allow to cool. Arrange the slices on plates, and spoon the tomato mixture onto each. Serve immediately.

ANOTHER WAY

If you prefer a more substantial bruschetta, cut the bread into 1.5 cm (¾ in) slices. Replace the basil with coriander, and add a little finely chopped chilli for a spicy alternative. You could also add diced pepper or chopped olives to the mixture.

Bacon-Wrapped Mushrooms

These ever-popular party hors d'oeuvres are quickly made in a halogen oven.

16 mushrooms
1 large mozzarella ball, cut into
16 pieces
16 strips bacon
1 tbsp olive oil

Makes 16

Clean the mushrooms and remove the stalks. Fill the centre of each mushroom with a piece of mozzarella. Wrap each mushroom with a strip of bacon and secure with a toothpick. Rub the mushrooms with a little olive oil.

To cook, place directly on the low rack of the halogen oven for 14 minutes at 200°C (400°F), turning them over after the first 7 minutes of cooking. Serve immediately.

ANOTHER WAY

Use chicken liver pâté instead of mozzarella to stuff the mushrooms.

Popcorn

Low-fat, high-fibre and so much fun to make in your halogen oven, this is one recipe you'll use time and time again.

200 g (8 oz) popping corn

Serves 4

Preheat the round tray to 250°C (480°F) and cook the popping corn on the tray on the low shelf of the halogen oven for 8 minutes. Leave to rest in the oven for 5 minutes to ensure all of the corn has popped (a few may not pop). Remove and decant into a serving bowl. Serve plain, or with one of the toppings listed below.

NOW TRY THIS...

SWEET MAPLE SAUCE

In the base of a small heatproof bowl place 50 g (2 oz) brown sugar, 2 tbsp maple syrup and 1 tbsp butter. Place this on the round oven tray on the low rack in the halogen oven. Cook the sauce at 250°C (480°F) for 3½ minutes. Remove and set aside. Use an oven glove to hold the bowl still, and whisk the sauce with a fork for a full 2 minutes until the ingredients are fully mixed to form the maple sauce. Pour over popcorn while still warm, or use as a dipping sauce.

SIMON AND GARFUNKEL

Pound together 1 tsp each dried parsley, sage, rosemary and thyme. Sprinkle herb powder over the hot popcorn.

HOTCORN

Mix together 2 tsp cayenne pepper, 2 tsp paprika and 1 tsp garlic powder. Sprinkle over hot popcorn.

POPCORN–MARSHMALLOW BAR

After popping your corn, mix 25 g (1 oz) marshmallows with 1 tbsp butter and melt in a heatproof bowl in the halogen oven. Combine melted marshmallow–butter mixture with popcorn, press into a greased baking tin and leave to cool for 10 minutes. Cut into 12 bars.

POPPY ROAD

Melt 75 g (3 oz) milk chocolate over a pan of simmering water on the hob, and mix with 2 tbsp glacé cherries, 2 tbsp sultanas and 2 tbsp chopped pecans. Mix the popcorn in. Drop spoonfuls of the mixture onto a baking sheet and leave to cool.

COLOURED CORN

If you want to make coloured popcorn, melt a small knob of butter on the round tray. Add 2–3 drops food colouring to the butter, then add the popping corn kernels.

Chocolate Brownies

These cake-like brownies are crunchy on the outside, because they are cooked on both sides, while being soft and chewy in the middle.

150 g (6 oz) butter
175 g (7 oz) dark chocolate
3 eggs
100 g (4 oz) dark brown sugar
25 g (1 oz) chocolate powder
   (such as Nesquick)
2 tbsp coffee liqueur
50 g (2 oz) flour

Serves 6

Line a 20 cm (8 in) round oven tray and a 20 cm (8 in) steamer tray (or a second oven tray) with baking paper. Using a little of the butter, grease both pieces of paper.

Add a cup of boiling water to the base of the halogen oven. Place the chocolate in a heatproof bowl. Place the remaining butter on top. Place the bowl on the low rack and cook at 200°C (400°F) for 5 minutes. Stir to combine the chocolate and butter, cook for 2 minutes more, then remove the bowl and stir again. Leave the boiling water in the base of the halogen oven.

Whisk the eggs and sugar together in a large bowl. Add the chocolate powder, melted chocolate mixture and coffee liqueur. Stir to combine, then fold in the flour. Pour the brownie mixture into the prepared round tray. Place the tray on the low rack and bake at 160°C (320°F) for 20 minutes. Remove, then place the lined steamer tray over the top of the part-cooked brownie and turn over, keeping the brownie sandwiched between the two round trays. Put it back into the halogen oven and cook for a further 15 minutes at 175°C (350°F) to cook the base, which is now facing up. Once cooked, remove from oven, turn back over, slice and serve hot with cream or ice cream.

ANOTHER WAY

To make extra-indulgent chocolate-iced brownies, mix together:
250 g (10 oz) icing sugar
100 g (4 oz) unsalted butter at
   room temperature
2 tbsp cocoa powder
½ tsp. vanilla extract
1 tbsp whole milk
Spread the icing on top of
the brownies, and leave to set
before serving.

Lavender Shortbread Cookies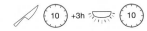

Shortbread-style sugar cookies are a popular treat with children, and ideal for making in the halogen oven. The subtle flavour of lavender gives a fashionable twist to an old favourite.

250 g (10 oz) unsalted butter, softened, plus extra for greasing
100 g (4 oz) sugar
60 g (2½ oz) icing sugar
1 large egg, lightly beaten
1 tbsp freeze-dried dehydrated lavender flowers, crushed to a powder
250 g (10 oz) flour
1 tsp bicarbonate of soda
1 tsp cream of tartar
pinch nutmeg

Makes about 50

In a large bowl, with an electric mixer, cream the butter and sugars together until light and fluffy. Beat in the egg and the crushed lavender. Sift together the flour, bicarbonate of soda and cream of tartar, and stir into the creamed mixture. Chill for 2–3 hours or overnight.

Grease the oven tray with a little butter. Roll out about a quarter of the cookie dough on a floured surface to 6 mm (¼ in) thickness, and cut out with a 5 cm (2 in) cookie cutter. Place on the oven tray and cook in the halogen oven on the high rack at 150°C (300°F) for 10 minutes. Turn off the oven and leave the cookies in the oven for 3 minutes. Then remove the tray from the oven and let the cookies cool on the tray for 3 minutes, before transferring them to a wire rack to cool completely. Wash and dry the oven tray. Repeat until you have used up all the dough. Cool on a wire rack and store in an airtight container.

ANOTHER WAY

If you cannot find lavender flowers, or lavender-flavoured sugar, use both 1 tsp vanilla extract and 1 tsp almond extract instead. Divide the dough and keep the rest covered and chilled in the refrigerator. Roll out only a quarter of the dough at a time, and work quickly, as the dough will get sticky as it warms up.

Cherry Kuchen

This is a quickly prepared, moist cherry cake, rich with butter and vanilla flavours, and delicious served with coffee, warm or cold, on its own or as part of a brunch buffet.

100 g (4 oz) unsalted butter,
   softened
100 g (4 oz) sugar
1 large egg
100 g (4 oz) flour
½ tsp baking powder
1 tsp vanilla extract
a little milk, if needed
450 g (1 lb) tin dark cherry
   pie filling
2 tbsp sliced almonds
icing sugar, to serve

Serves 6

In a large bowl, beat the first six ingredients together to make a fairly thick batter. If the batter seems too thick, thin it with a little milk. Pour most of the batter into the bottom of a greased 20 cm (8 in) tin. Pour the cherry pie filling on top, and drop the remaining batter on top of the cherries. Scatter the sliced almonds on top. Bake on the low rack at 150°C (300°F) for 20 minutes, turn the heat up to 160° (325°F) and cook for 20 minutes, or until golden brown and cooked through. Cool in the pan for 5 minutes before cutting into 6 slices. Dust with icing sugar.

NOW TRY THIS...

APRICOT AND ALMOND KUCHEN

Prepare the basic recipe, adding 1 tsp almond extract to the batter. Instead of the cherry filling, drain 1 tin apricots. Heat juice with 2 tbsp cornflour and 2 tbsp orange juice until boiling and thickened. Chop apricots, add to the juice and cool before using.

PLUM KUCHEN

Prepare the basic recipe, omitting the cherries. Substitute 450 g (1 lb) pitted and chopped plums, stewed gently in a little water and a little sugar to taste. Cool before using.

APPLE AND CINNAMON KUCHEN

Prepare the basic recipe, replacing the butter with 200 ml (8 fl oz) vegetable oil. Instead of the cherry filling, stew 2 peeled and sliced apples with 2 tbsp sugar and 2 tsp cinnamon. Cool before using.

RHUBARB AND ORANGE KUCHEN

Prepare the basic recipe, omitting the cherries. Substitute 450 g (1 lb) sliced rhubarb, stewed in a little orange juice and sugar to taste. Cool before using.

Apricot and Ginger Upside Down Cake

This wonderfully sticky cake is great with afternoon coffee, or with cream for a delicious dessert.

Sponge Mix
75 g (3 oz) plain flour
2 tsp baking powder
100 g (4 oz) butter
2 eggs
50 g (2 oz) caster sugar

Base
3 tbsp maple syrup
1 tbsp butter
25 g (1 oz) crystallised ginger
5 candied cherries
1 400 g (14 oz) tin apricot
  halves, drained
butter, for greasing

Serves 5

Mix sponge ingredients in a food mixer or in a large bowl with a wooden spoon until creamed together. Divide the maple syrup, butter, candied cherries, stem ginger and apricots between 5 ramekins greased with butter. Place the cake mix on top.

Place 1 cm (½ in) water in the base of the halogen oven. Place the ramekins in the halogen oven on the lower rack. Cook at 160°C (325°F) for 45–55 minutes or until a skewer inserted comes out clean. Turn out when cooked, upside down, on a plate.

NOW TRY THIS...

PINEAPPLE UPSIDE DOWN CAKE

Prepare the basic recipe, omitting the ginger and replacing the glacé cherries and apricot halves with 1 400-g (14-oz) can pineapple chunks.

PLUM UPSIDE DOWN CAKE

Prepare the basic recipe, substituting 300 g (12 oz) plums, stewed in a little water, with 3 tbsp maple syrup for the apricot base.

APRICOT AND ALMOND UPSIDE DOWN CAKE

Prepare the basic recipe, omitting the ginger. When cooked, turn out the cakes and sprinkle with toasted flaked almonds.

SPICED PEAR UPSIDE DOWN CAKE

Peel, core and quarter 6 ripe pears. Place in a medium-sized pan with 400 ml (16 fl oz) red wine, 2 tbsp soft brown sugar, 1 cinnamon stick and 1 vanilla pod. Simmer gently for 30–40 minutes, or until the pears are tender. Drain the juice and use the pears in place of the apricot mix. The pear juice can be reduced, sweetened and used as a sauce.

Marsala and Amaretto Peaches

Peaches are quite often a little difficult to catch right at that moment when they are ripe, soft and succulent. So when they are a little hard, bake them in sweet marsala wine, and serve very cold with chilled mascarpone and fromage frais, mixed with honey.

4 firm but ripe peaches
250 ml (8 fl oz) marsala wine
2 tbsp amaretto liqueur
4 tbsp sugar
2 tbsp honey
1 tsp cornflour
2 tsp water
4 tbsp mascarpone
4 tbsp fromage frais or Greek
    yogurt
3 tbsp honey

Serves 4

Halve the peaches, remove the pits and place the peaches in a large bowl. Cover with boiling water, leave for 1 minute, drain and slide the skins off. Place them in a shallow baking dish. In a medium bowl, mix the marsala with the amaretto, sugar and honey, and pour it over the peaches. Bake, uncovered, on the low rack at 160°C (325°F) for 25–30 minutes. Remove from the halogen oven and set aside to cool for 10 minutes.

Place the peaches on a serving dish, cover and place in the refrigerator. Pour the wine and sugar syrup into a small saucepan. Bring to the boil. In a small bowl, mix the cornflour with the water, and add it to the syrup, stirring, until it thickens. Set aside to cool, then pour it over the peaches. Chill until really cold, about 6 hours.

In a medium bowl, mix the mascarpone, fromage frais and honey, until well combined. Cover and chill until required.

Serve 2 peach halves per person, with the sauce spooned over, and mascarpone mix on the side.

ANOTHER WAY

For a nice variation, replace the peaches with unpeeled nectarines. Add 1 tbsp mascarpone and 2 tsp light brown sugar to each nectarine half, pour 75 ml (3 fl oz) peach schnapps around the nectarines and bake as per the recipe.

Chocolate Rum Bananas

These are easy to prepare in advance for a dinner party. Your guests will love the taste of the melted chocolate with the gooey banana.

2 tbsp dark brown sugar
2 tbsp rum
4 bananas
12 milk chocolate squares
4 scoops vanilla ice cream

Serves 4

Cut 4 (30 cm/12 in) squares of foil. Mix the sugar and rum together. Peel the bananas and place each one on a square of foil. Cut along the length of each banana to form a pocket. Fill the pocket with 3 chocolate squares and sprinkle with the sugared rum. Close the foil to form a tight pouch and cook on the low rack in the halogen oven at 260°C (500°F) for 10 minutes.

Carefully remove the bananas from their pouches and place them on serving plates. Serve hot with a scoop of ice cream.

ANOTHER WAY

To make this for kids, replace the rum with hot chocolate. To make a healthier variation you could also use raisins or sultanas instead of chocolate squares.

Baked Apples

This is such a nice warming dessert in winter with cream poured over the top. In the summer, serve the apples with ice cream.

4 cooking apples
75 g (3 oz) raisins
1 tbsp brown sugar
½ tsp ground cinnamon
2 tbsp maple syrup
1 tbsp butter

Serves 4

Core the apples and peel a little around the top, making a bigger hole. Set them on the round oven tray. In a small bowl, mix the raisins, brown sugar and cinnamon. Stuff the apples with the mixture. Drizzle all over with the maple syrup, then place a bit of butter on each apple.

Place the tray on the low rack of the halogen oven and cook at 160°C (325°F) for 35 minutes. Remove and serve hot.

ANOTHER WAY

Add 40 g (1½ oz) chopped pecans or walnuts or chopped dried apricots and only 40 g (1½ oz) raisins to the filling for a change.

Chocolate Bread Pudding with Irish Cream Sauce

The title of this dessert just does not do it justice. This is a chocolate, praline and cream, succulent and gooey extravaganza, a sweet to inspire poets.

Irish Cream Sauce
250 ml (8 fl oz) whipping cream
4 tbsp Irish cream liqueur
2 tbsp sugar
1 tsp vanilla extract
1 tsp cornflour
2 tsp water

Bread Puddings
butter for greasing
3 large eggs
40 g (1½ oz) sugar, plus more for sprinkling
2 tsp vanilla extract
400 ml (14 fl oz) whipping cream
80 ml (3 fl oz) whole milk
400 g (14 oz) 1.5 cm (¾ in) cubes of French bread
100 g (4 oz) dark chocolate, finely chopped
100 g (4 oz) praline-filled milk chocolate, chopped

Serves 6

Make the sauce. In a medium saucepan over a medium heat, bring the cream, liqueur, sugar and vanilla to the boil. In a small bowl, mix the cornflour and water to a paste, and whisk into the cream mixture. Simmer gently for 3 minutes until thickened, stirring continuously. Remove from the heat, cool and transfer to a small bowl. Chill in the refrigerator for at least 2 hours.

Grease 6 ramekins (10 cm/4 in in diameter) with a little butter.

Make the bread puddings. In a large bowl, whisk together the eggs, sugar, vanilla, 250 ml (8 fl oz) cream and milk. Add the bread and chocolates and stir to combine. Leave to stand for 30 minutes, stirring occasionally. Divide the mixture equally between the ramekins, and drizzle with the remaining cream. Sprinkle each one with a little sugar, and bake on the low rack at 175°C (350°F) for 20 minutes, or until slightly golden and the custard is set. If the top looks like it is darkening too much, turn the heat down to 150°C (300°F) for the last 5–10 minutes. Leave to stand for 10 minutes, then serve the dessert warm, with the chilled sauce.

ANOTHER WAY

Substitute white chocolate for the praline-filled milk chocolate and challah for the French bread. Add 50 g (2 oz) dried cherries to the mixture before soaking.

Lemon Delight

This very lemony dessert separates as it cooks into a sponge with a lemon sauce underneath.

6 tbsp unsalted butter, plus
    extra for greasing
50 g (2 oz) sugar
zest and juice from 1¹/₂ lemons
1 rounded tbsp flour
2 eggs, separated
just under 160 ml (6 fl oz) milk
icing sugar, to serve

Serves 4

Grease 4 ramekins (7.5–10 cm/3–4 in diameter) with a little butter. Place a shallow baking tin on the low rack of the halogen oven and pour in enough water to cover the base.

In a medium bowl, cream the remaining butter and sugar with the lemon zest until pale and creamy. Add the flour and lemon juice, and mix well. In a separate bowl, whisk the egg yolks with the milk, then whisk the mixture slowly, a little at a time, into the butter–sugar mixture. Whisk the egg whites with an electric mixer until firm, not stiff, and fold into the batter.

Divide the mixture between the ramekins and place on the baking tin. Bake at 175°C (350°F) for 10 minutes, then turn the heat down to 160°C (325°F) and cook for 15 minutes, or until the top has turned a golden brown and the bottom has set. Sprinkle with icing sugar and serve immediately.

ANOTHER WAY

Serve with fresh raspberries and whipped cream for a stunning dessert. For a change, use orange juice and orange zest instead of lemon. For a sophisticated dinner party dessert, replace 1 tbsp of the milk with orange liqueur.

Cherry and Chocolate Cobbler

Chocolate desserts are always a winner, especially with children. This one, like most, is delicious served with vanilla ice cream.

100 g (4 oz) butter, softened,
    plus a little for greasing
50 g (2 oz) sugar
1 large egg
100 g (4 oz) flour
1 tbsp unsweetened cocoa
    powder
1 tsp baking powder
pinch salt
1 tsp vanilla extract
1 (450 g/16 oz) tin cherry pie
    filling
a little milk, if needed
icing sugar and vanilla ice
    cream, to serve

Serves 8

Grease 8 ramekins (7.5–10 cm/3–4 in diameter) with a little butter.

In a medium bowl, whisk together the butter, sugar, egg, flour, cocoa powder, baking powder, salt and vanilla to make a thick batter. If it seems too stiff, thin it with a little milk.

Divide ⅔ of the batter between the ramekins, then spoon on the cherry pie filling, dividing it equally between the dishes. Spoon on the rest of the batter.

Cook 4 ramekins at a time, on the low rack of the halogen oven, at 155°C (315°F) for about 20 minutes, or until the cobbler has set. Remove from the oven, and keep warm while you cook the remaining ramekins. Sprinkle with icing sugar, and serve warm with vanilla ice cream.

ANOTHER WAY

For a healthier option, substitute vegetable oil for the butter.

To vary the flavours you can substitute other fruit pie fillings for the cherry, or use a fruit compote made by lightly cooking together a selection of fruits and berries with a little sugar until they are soft and blended together.

INDEX